OUR SUMMER WITH THE ESKIMOS

☞

6524 NE 181st St., Suite 2, Kenmore, WA 98028

Epicenter Press is a regional press publishing nonfiction books about the arts, history, environment, and diverse cultures and lifestyles of Alaska and the Pacific Northwest.
For more information, visit www.EpicenterPress.com

Text © 2021 Constance Helmericks

Photographs by Constance & Harmon Helmericks
Provided and corrected by Jean Aspen

Cover photos by Constance & Harmon Helmericks

Cover and interior design by Scott Book & Melisssa Vail Coffman

All rights reserved. No part of this publication may be reproduced, stored in a retrieval system, or transmitted in any form by any means, electronic, mechanical, photocopying, recording, or otherwise, without the prior written permission of the publisher. Permission is given for brief excerpts to be published with book reviews in newspaper, magazines, newsletters, catalogs, and online publications.

ISBN: 978-1-941890-38-7 (Trade Paperback)

ISBN: 978-1-941890-39-4 (Ebook)

Library of Congress Control Number: 2020934470

To the Eskimos

Books by Constance Helmericks

We Live in Alaska, 1944, Epicenter Press 2019
We Live in the Arctic, 1947, Epicenter Press 2021
Our Summer with the Eskimos, 1948, Epicenter Press 2021
Our Alaskan Winter, 1949, Epicenter Press 2021
Flight of the Arctic Tern, 1952, Epicenter Press 2018
Down the Wild River North, 1969, Epicenter Press 2017
Hunting in North America, 1956
Australian Adventure, 1972

Books by Jean Aspen

Arctic Daughter: a Wilderness Journey, 1988, 2015
Arctic Son: Fulfilling the Dream, 1995, 2014
A Child of Air (a novel), 2008
Trusting the River, Epicenter Press 2017

Documentaries by Jean Aspen and Tom Irons

Arctic Son: Fulfilling the Dream, 2013
Arctic Daughter: A Lifetime of Wilderness, 2018
Rewilding Kernwood, 2019

OUR SUMMER WITH THE ESKIMOS

CONSTANCE HELMERICKS
& HARMON HELMERICKS

Epicenter Press

Kenmore

Contents

Preface ix
Foreword xiii
PART ONE *Breakup* 1
PART TWO *The Colville River* 39
PART THREE *Beechey Point* 103
PART FOUR *The Coming of Winter* 187
About the Author 201

Preface

Today is Earth Day. Beyond my tiny log shelter, Alaska's Brooks Range lies deep under snow at eleven below zero F°. The river, hard as stone, is incised with frozen tracks as migrating caribou head north to their calving grounds. I'm alone this April, saying goodbye to a way of life that has been home for me since my conception in these remote mountains. I watch the sleeping river and read my mother's books. For three years my husband, Tom Irons, and I have been taking down and rewilding all that we built here over the decades, removing our whimsical log structures and replanting their footprint with sod from the roofs. Tom will join me after the ice goes out, when a chartered plane can land on the river bar. By autumn only my books and our documentaries will remain to speak of the years we have loved this bend in the river. In late summer we will depart by canoe once more, a lingering farewell to our beautiful dream. There comes a point in every dream for letting go.

Connie Helmericks, my mother, died on Earth Day. She was 69—a year older than I am now. Earth Day seems fitting, for she was passionate about our living planet. Paradoxically, during the decade she and my father, Bud Helmericks, wandered the Arctic, she lived by hunting—as I once did, and for the same reason: it is how one survives afoot for years in this wild land. I recall my mother as a deeply sentimental woman who seemed misplaced in the culture of her day. If at moments she sounds too sure of herself, it is perhaps in defense of her gentle heart. When I catch her true voice, the tone is lyrical and sensitive—a love song for this great wilderness, a song that still rings in my heart.

Connie would write five best-selling books during her twenties, propelling my young parents into national acclaim and opening doors for documentaries, airplanes and lecture tours. It was heady stuff—a dream which would overshadow their future. In this third book, she and Bud continue a 26-month trek across the top of Alaska, spanning 1944 to 1946. After overwintering alone in the Brooks Range (as told in *We Live in the Arctic*), they descend the Alatna River in their homemade, fourteen-foot canoe, intent on crossing the Continental Divide and paddling down the unknown Colville River to the Arctic Ocean. The following year they will journey along the arctic coast and into Canada. Having never seen tundra—and ill-equipped for life in this treeless landscape—they hope to learn from nomadic Inuit families. Even after a year of living off the land, this is an audacious plan. No one can tell them about the barren grounds ahead, and there will be no exits beyond their own strengths.

Although "Inuit" is now preferred over "Eskimo" (and these families were more specifically Iñupiat), this edition remains true to her original book. I have done my best to clean the aging photos and write captions for a window into their lost world. Connie's education in literature and sociology made her an excellent witness to the humanity of these free people caught in the crosshairs of change. Considering that she lived in a time when "primitive" cultures and women were considered inferior, Connie writes of the Iñupiat with humor, insight, and affection, transcending stereotypes to depict them as individuals whom we grow to know and love. If she seems to cover the ground a bit defensively at times, it helps to recall the biases of her day.

I once asked her why she had shifted to Bud's perspective in this and her subsequent book. "In traditional Eskimo culture," she told me, "women and men had very different roles. It wasn't acceptable for me to travel with the hunters, so your father's life was more interesting than mine."

What did the Iñupiat think of my parents? We'll never know, for they didn't write books and would not have passed judgement anyway. From my experience, Native cultures are careful not to infringe. The closest one may get to advice is, "My daughter thinks she sees sea ice." From this you must deduce that a wise traveler would remain in camp today.

Life was hard for these scattered people, and their traditional roles helped them survive. Starvation was an accepted fact, for there was no safety net beyond the generosity of other families who might also be hungry. They had never been numerous, and now a third of their scattered community had died of influenza—whole families decimated. Connie reports that young hunters were scarce (many probably drafted into World War II), and the remaining men undertook feeding those who had no hunter. Nevertheless, these gracious people welcomed my parents, made skin clothing for them, and taught them how to travel, find food, and build shelters. Had the Iñupiat families not befriended strangers from a different world, my parents would never have survived their first winter on the tundra and I would not have been born. My early childhood was grounded in these generous families, happily eating from their communal pot and wearing fur clothing which Nannie, my "Eskimo Grandmother," made for me.

Connie's next book, *Our Alaskan Winter* completes this remarkable odyssey. As arctic darkness closes down, she and Bud follow the nomadic hunting life with a wild young man and his dogs. As you read, think of my young mother left on the tundra without so much as a sleeping bag, sitting cross-legged on caribou skins in a snow-banked tent. She is bent over her lap, writing three books in a meticulous hand by the light of a kerosene lantern. Outside the sky arches vast and pastel, blending with a ground fog where snow twinkles into dunes like sand and the wind never ceases. Think of her carrying three handwritten manuscripts bound in caribou hide by foot, dogsled, and canoe those many months across the top of Alaska and finally along the Arctic Ocean into Canada.

Jean Aspen, Brooks Range wilderness, Alaska
April 22, 2018
www.jeanaspen.com

Connie Helmericks, age 26

Foreword

One summer Bud and I set out together in our homemade canoe, the *Little Willow*, to follow the Koyukuk, a tributary of the Yukon, into the unexplored Brooks Range of arctic Alaska. For a year we lived there in the Brooks Range, on wild meat when our food gave out, seeing no other human beings. Our experience of building our own log cabin and living there near the edge of timber line, high on the Arctic Divide, two hundred and forty miles by river from our nearest known neighbors, is told in *We Live in the Arctic*, which ends with breakup of the river ice the following spring.

But we wanted to go still farther in our canoe the next summer—as far, in fact, as the shores of the Arctic Ocean. The present book, *Our Summer with the Eskimos*, takes us down the thousand-mile-long treeless Colville River into the world of the Eskimos. Here, along the rim of the continent, our canoe played hide-and-seek with the polar ice pack and we learned the lore of getting food and shelter in a land of no fuel and no landmarks. The volume to follow, *Our Alaskan Winter*, will describe our life of hunting in order to live, and our wandering Eskimo friends. Here we had no house, but lived in tent-igloos for a year until at last we canoed our way, the third summer, along the coast of the Arctic Ocean from Alaska to Canada, securing airplane transportation back to civilization from Aklavik in Canada's Mackenzie delta. All of these books were written while in the arctic, sitting on a floor of caribou skins, by the light of a coal-oil lantern, far from the world of today.

Constance Helmericks

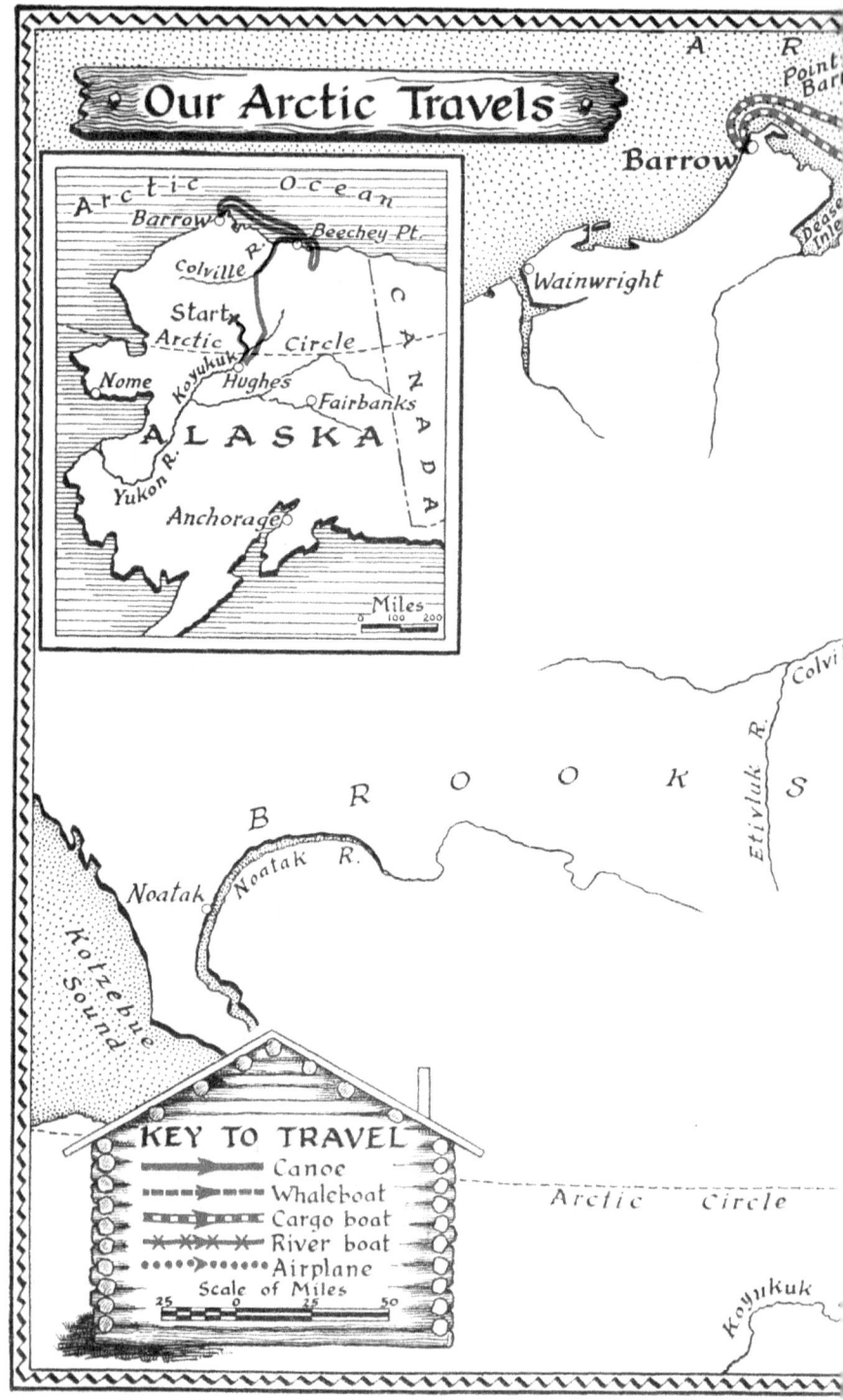

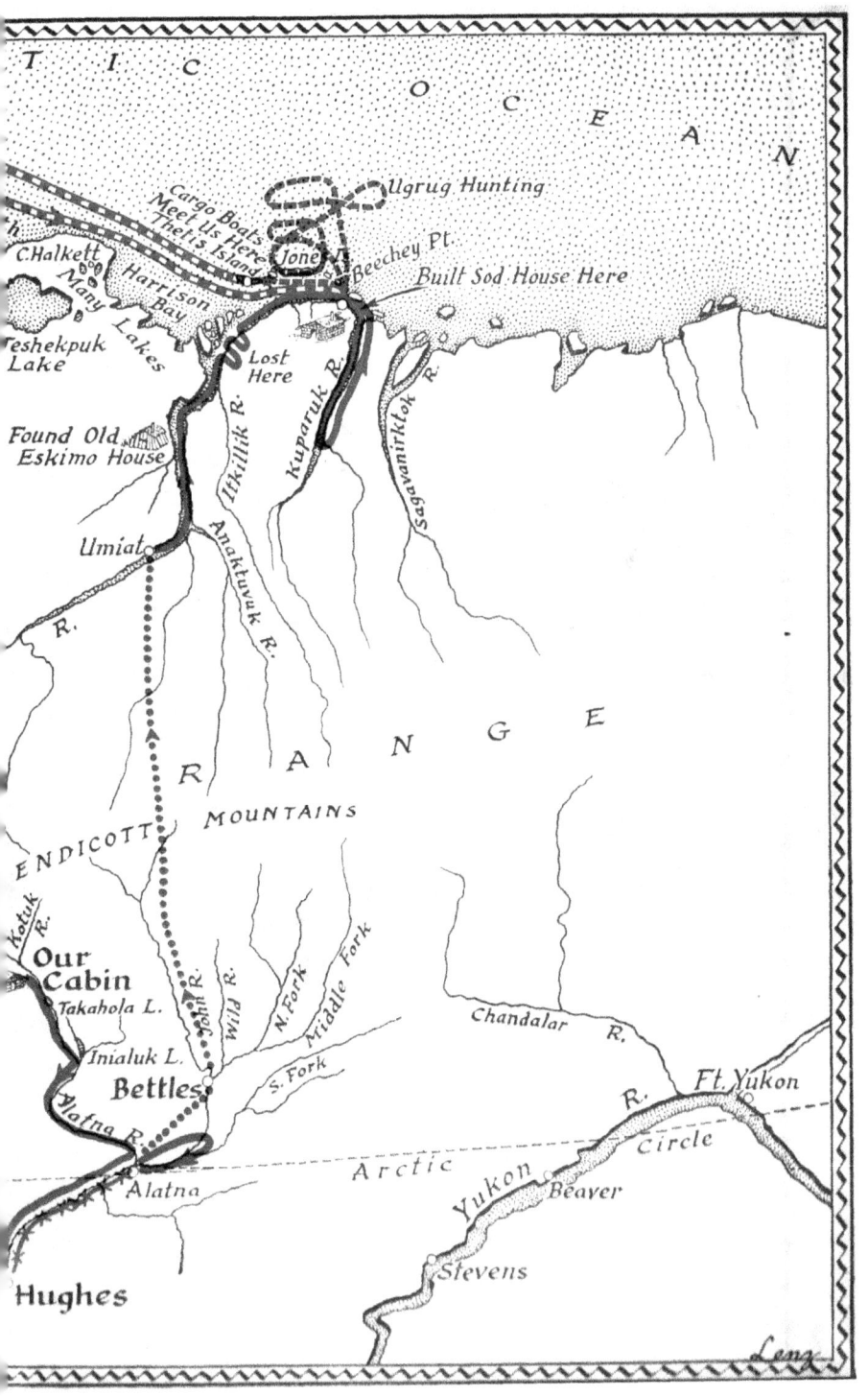

Bud and Connie in summer dress

PART ONE

Breakup

Mosquitoes probe Bud's shirt

Connie peeks from our tent among the flowers

1

The new year should really begin with spring break up in the arctic. It is then that the seasons and life in the North leap forward anew. The change comes overnight. Last week snow lay deep and chill winds blew. This week the river is swollen with melted snow and frosted with floating ice. The air vibrates with bird songs while bluebottle flies crowd one another for a warm spot in the sun. The snowshoes are put away and the old canoe comes down from the cache. And in enclosed mountain fastnesses the spruce forest of Alaska whispers of a new place that is far away. It always whispers that way in spring. Some people call this spring fever.

Yes, there had been lean times and uncertain times, but all in all it had been a happy year.[1] We hadn't seen another human being for ten months. We had run out of grub, and at the present time we were living on fish and spring birds. Alone here in the Endicott Mountains of the great arctic Brooks Range, it had been our river, our valley, and our world. But with spring breakup we were starting another year of wandering. We were leaving the forest for the prairie north to the coastal plains. It would be new being a plainsman! There was a green land up there beneath a sun which never sets in the summertime, a land which few white men have ever seen to this day.

How we would get there was a problem yet to solve. Our first

---

1 See *We Live in the Arctic*.

step was to get out down this river on which we had wintered to the village of Alatna on the Koyukuk River—north of the Arctic Circle, five hundred river miles north of the Yukon, this village lies—but we were headed farther north still. Soon at Alatna village we would see people, hear the news, read our mail. How would salt taste to us? How would it seem to discard our rags for new clothes? Who was President of the United States now? What was the news of this our land, Alaska? All these questions and many like them would be answered for two Alaskans when we brought our furs in to the trading post.

The river had reached its flood peak and held steady before our cabin door. I tried to stretch a pint of linseed oil over the canvas bottom of our canoe, the *Little Willow*, with some success, while Connie held a wash day. Ducks sported about in the swollen backwaters of the arctic mountain river as we let the *Little Willow* into the water. For some reason or other I am always amazed when a canoe floats, no matter how many times I have been in one. Or perhaps I don't always trust my own constructions. Down the icy trail we trundled our belongings, and once again that huge pile of duffel went into our homemade fourteen-foot canoe—another miracle to Connie. We cut a good supply of dry firewood for the next person who might someday come by this way, took down the stovepipe so it wouldn't rust out through the years, boarded up the windows with our old ax-hewn table top a precaution against bears and tacked a welcome note on the door. This last was hardly necessary, for a traveler this far off the beaten track is always welcome. But somehow it made us feel better. We carried the last bundle to the waiting canoe, and all was ready. All except one thing: we had to say good-by to our log cabin. We had packed almost regretfully, for we were leaving a home and all our friends behind us most likely forever.

It was a funny thing about that arctic mountain valley the most peaceful place I have ever been. We might have starved when we ran out of food, but we always felt safe. We had been lucky arctic hunters.

Inside the cabin the sunlight made little bars upon the floor where it came between the boards that covered the windows. It all seemed so hushed and still, as if already forgotten and alone. When I closed the door, Connie began to cry. "It's all been so lovely," she said. "All ours, the things you would never dream that we found in the arctic, and I have been so happy here."

Five days later, when we stepped ashore at Alatna, the muddy, turbulent river waters, surging with strength from melted snow, were lashing and undercutting the toppling banks. I helped Connie up the incline in our stiff, cold, rubber hip boots.

We asked the Indian children where the missionaries were. They apparently didn't know, and suggested they might have gone downtown. This puzzled us, for to us "downtown" had always meant where the business center of any city was. Here we found it meant the half of town that lay downstream, while the upstream half was, logically enough, "uptown."

We knocked on the mission house door, but apparently it was deserted.

It had taken us five weeks to get up the Alatna River into the Brooks Range the year before, and now five days to come back down it, I reflected as we lamely started downtown.

"Look, footprints of white women's shoes! We can track them down!" said Connie.

Sure enough, there were the footprints of the two missionary ladies as plain as could be in the mud, heading for the airport. We followed past a few log cabins by the river front and finally squeezed by another one, for the river was actually flowing under one corner of the cabin. The trail led on down-river and to the airport.

The airport was a gravel bar of the Koyukuk River. In high water the river rose over the bar and left driftwood stranded. Here we found the two missionary women just returning after clearing the driftwood off the bar so that tomorrow's mail plane could land.

We four white people approached each other wonderingly. With a few last hurried steps, Connie and I gripped once again hands we had shaken a summer ago.

"You are the first human beings we've seen to shake hands with," said Connie, "since we left you at this spot last year." "We've scarcely seen a white person either," they said. It was a fine moment for all of us.

In Alatna again, Bud takes our canoe apart

Our outfit is gradually shuttled to Bettles

2

"How is the war?"
"Over in Germany! Good gracious, didn't you know?"
"No, of course we didn't know. How could we?" I asked.
"Oh, didn't you have a radio with you? We thought you did. Then" they looked at us "you don't know anything?"

"No," we said. "Tell us."

So, they told us about the fall of the European dictatorships and that President Roosevelt was dead; rather stunning news all of it, and we got it in one dose.

"But don't just stand there. Come into the house and rest, and we'll tell you all the details of everything out in the world." The two ladies seized our arms. "We'll talk while you're eating. You must be very tired after a whole year of exploring! We have your room all ready for you. It has been waiting with new curtains for a month. You will want to bathe."

Connie and I looked embarrassed. Miss Hill helped Connie out of her parka jacket, which, seen inside a civilized house, very likely made the missionary nurse want to wash her hands after touching it. It did not seem right to hang our things on the white wall, so we put them on the floor in a corner inconspicuously. Then we asked what day of the week it was and what date, and learned that we were a few days off in our calculations, as we had had no calendar for the new year. Inside the mission house we were to learn once again the meaning of

Alaskan hospitality. With a scurrying for hot water and pitchers and basins, and running upstairs and down for spotless linens and thick Turkish towels, a rattling of pans and stuffing of wood into the cooking range, and everybody talking at once and bumping into each other in excitement! Connie and I sat in a daze of gratitude, never imagining that our arrival could cause such commotion anywhere.

Milk was set before us in immaculate glasses tinkling with cracked ice. But we didn't remember ordinary water glasses as appearing so small and so fragile. We took them up carefully. Yes, we had waited for this moment for a long time. The milk tasted strange and delicious but not at all as we had remembered it. Actually, if a person has been living for long on game alone, it takes several days for a constitutional change to take place in the enzymes of the mouth and stomach, as well as in the internal bacteria which influence digestion, so that he can again handle a mixed civilized diet. We drank the milk and then were each given a red apple.

I broke mine in two and ate it in four bites, core, stem, and all, and looked around to see if anything else went with it. Nothing else apparently did, so I leaned back and tried to contemplate civilized life. The food didn't seem real. The apples were soft. Maybe we had developed powerful jaws this year from eating that eight-hundred-pound grizzly bear along with our several moose and caribou. The ladies were setting the table with more dishes with insignificant little dabs of things in them than I had ever seen in my life. Such tiny spoons and saucers! Had we, too, once found a teaspoon satisfactory for conveying something to the mouth, and really got fed that way? Table knives looked like dull, useless ornaments.

How do people cut meat with those things? The answer is that people who do must expect their meat to be awfully soft and insipid. What a great part color and the appeal to the eye play in the civilized person's menu I had forgotten. People eat foods of certain colors that go well together. Our table was just like a rainbow. Such are one's first impressions on "coming back."

We all stayed up talking most of the night, and even after retirement I don't think a soul in that house slept a wink. The ladies put Connie in the little room which they had prepared for her upstairs, and relegated me with less ceremony to an adjoining storehouse, for no man could sleep on these premises.

Our mail, which the ladies had saved for us in the post office, was enormous. When your mail piles up for a year, it makes something. We looked forward to reading it with mixed joy and foreboding, for mail brings bad news sometimes as well as good. We were lucky, though, and our families and friends were all right. Miss Hill and Miss Kay gave us the use of their private study, and here we wrote our families. We had often wondered how our Koyukuk friend old Bill, the prospector, and Little Miss Muffet, his pet cat, had made out the winter. Bill and Miss Muffet had been left at a spot above Old Man River where Bill intended to build a cabin. We had said good-by to him there last summer. Bill was so old and feeble with his heart trouble that we had wondered at his courage to live all alone. But then old Bill had not been out of Alaska for forty years and he knew no other life.

The missionaries had tried to persuade the old prospector to come and live near Alatna, so they could look after him, but he liked his life along the Koyukuk and declined their kind offers in order to be where he hoped to find gold. The missionaries had then instructed all the natives to always stop and see how old Bill was and help him. Some of the natives helped Bill with his cabin and cut firewood for his sheet-iron stove. Bill was to live in his tent until his cabin should be completed.

Late in the fall a native came to Miss Hill in alarm. Miss Hill took a trip at once in the mission boat—running her own outboard motor twelve miles down the river to Bill's residence. There had been a fire. She found the old man lying inside the burned tent, dead. His clothing was badly burned, and his belongings were scattered about in a circle outside the tent as if he had tried to save his things from the fire by throwing them out.

In such situations the nearest commissioner must be notified. He either then comes to investigate or he may appoint someone to make the investigation. Miss Hill was asked by radio telephone if she would take charge. Upon closer examination she found that Bill had shot himself with his rifle. There, scattered about, were many empty shell cases. It appeared, then, that old Bill probably was asleep in his tent when that calamity had occurred against which every camper must be eternally on guard: his tent had caught fire. When he awoke it was doubtless burning fiercely. The old Alaskan had attempted to save his grubstake and had been badly burned. He then tried to signal someone by firing his rifle. When no one came, and he saw there was no hope of rescue from freezing, he had held his .30-30 between his knees and pointed it at himself. What became of Miss Muffet, his pet kitten, was unknown, but it was surmised he had killed her before killing himself. He shot himself with his last shell.

3

The thermometer which three days ago sank to the twenties now rose to the seventies by midday, while gone from the lowlands was the last trace of rotting snow. The motor of our canoe turned over in a steady rhythm while we relaxed, drifting down the burnished platter of the Koyukuk River, gazing on earth and grass. We had to go down into the edge of the Temperate Zone to trade our furs.

At the village of Hughes presently we found Les and Mrs. James, running around the side of their house to welcome us. Mrs. James was painting a new white picket fence about the yard. She had whipsawed the pieces herself and turned modern landscape gardener. The Jameses had just completed their own private airport and were going to buy a plane. Les was doing wonders for the country with his new D-4 Caterpillar. "Have you eaten?" was the first question the lone white couple asked us.

"Heck no! I wouldn't spoil my appetite with Hughes at the other end of the trail!"

"Did you get us the new motor we ordered for our canoe, Les?" This was the question I dreaded to ask and the answer I didn't want to hear came back: No.

A few hours later found me flying in to Fairbanks on the mail plane with our old motor under my arm, for I intended to either see personally that it was fixed or get a new one. A taxi took me downtown to the hotel. I ordered a meal again at a restaurant and walked down a paved street. People were rushing around. and I wondered why the hurry. In the course of a couple of days I argued an old dealer out of two motors. He had them to sell, of course, but he hated to give them up. Convincing him of my need and of the integrity of my character was a job requiring patience. While I waited it occurred to me that I should get Connie and me a couple of passports here in town, in case we should go on into Canada this year, following the edge of the Arctic Ocean. Here would be my only chance to get any papers.

I found the United States Customs Office and wandered in.

Some men were talking about hunting—the usual topic. "What can I do for you?" asked one in a friendly, lazy way. I explained where I was going, and tried to explain why.

I didn't know exactly why, except that Connie and I had become arctic dwellers and to wander around seemed natural. At this the man called the other two men over and we talked about the American arctic some and they said they wished they could see it too, but they were too busy.

This was very irregular. There was no customs inspector or, well, any person at all, where Canada joins Alaska on the Arctic Ocean, they decided. "The only trouble will come for you when you enter the United States again, through Canada. But we will fix a paper that will take care of you," they said. "Hey, can you spell?"

"No," I said.

After they all shook hands with me and wished Connie and me good luck, I went over town to a ladies' dress shop to buy Connie a new nightgown. She had cautioned me about buying a silk gown or anything fancy. "Just a common flannel gown, warm, with long sleeves that will be comfortable in the sleeping bag," she had specified.

I found a store that sold women's apparel and wandered in.

I don't suppose I shall ever feel quite at ease in such a shop with those scantily dressed parts of plaster manikins and a bevy of sharp-looking clerks. Just my luck, I was the only customer, and seven feminine helpers clustered about me.

"I would like to see some ladies' nightgowns," I finally managed. There was a scuttle for boxes, and some lovely imported garments were shown me at once. They ranged in price from fifty dollars on up. I said they were lovely and then the clerks began telling each other how lovely they were, and one even tried holding a very sheer gown up to sort of model it on herself. I turned a shade pink and asked to see something —well, heavier or warmer. All the time I was trying to remember what kind of material Connie had asked for.

This last effort brought out the twenty-dollar bracket with about as many models as before. "No," I finally managed, feeling rather cheap, "some heavy material like well like my shirt here."

At this they all stopped chattering to peer at me. I turned another shade and tried to keep calm. Finally. one girl found the kind of gown I was looking for and I was too befuddled to ask price or size. I said I would take it. The entire staff formed a line to watch me as I beat a retreat.

With the new nightgown I lugged the new motors, the first a ten-horsepower rebuilt and the other a brand-new one and-a-half horse (the one we kept for ourselves), one under each arm, to the airline offices. Wein Airlines wanted me to pay for a charter trip in order to get back to Hughes. They had no pay load waiting as yet and would not have for two weeks. I couldn't pay charter—whew! That reminded me, Les had been crying for bacon for his Indians, and hadn't been able to get it. Therefore, I scoured the town for bacon and succeeded in buying up five hundred pounds for Les, and Wein's consented to convey me back at once at the regular passenger rate.

After helping load the bacon and roll out the plane, I got in, well satisfied with town life for the year. Within a short time. the pleasant northern city lay behind us and we were flying northwest over wide country once more through rain circles. Rain circles are rainbows that form a complete circle when viewed from the air; in and out of cloud banks whose lower sides were pierced by sharp mountain peaks our old Stinson labored, then over the green flats and Hughes on the Koyukuk, of another world, lay beneath us. The bottom of our freshly painted canoe flashed a welcome. in bright red as the airplane shot over it.

Connie had painted the *Little Willow* red because this summer we were going into a very big country and we wanted to be conspicuous along the edge of the Arctic Ocean should any pilot come looking for us there. The area of our solitary playground this year would be roughly about sixty thousand square miles wherein we would be the only white people.

The Koyukuk River looked like a toy with its many sloughs and islands as the plane circled over it and headed in for the landing strip.

A lake only a mile away was set by a single moose feeding upon water lilies in its exact center. "Yes," I thought, "the river looks like a toy from here, but how different it looks when you are taking your chances on it in a frail canoe!"

Quite a lot of people fly over Alaska these days and more will be flying in the future. The future of the whole arctic lies in the air. But how much could we, strangers, have learned about the real country beneath us by merely seeing it from above? After all, most of humanity still lives on the ground and it is with the ground that we have to deal.

The Koyukuk River had risen steadily with the thaws. When a river rises it picks up all the driftwood that it deposited when it last dropped. We had hoped to have a light canoe, but as it seemed likely that we would not be able to get clear gasoline (rather than aviation gas) northward from Hughes, we stocked up with fifty gallons of gas, which weighed, roughly, four hundred pounds. This weight, combined with fifty pounds of dried and condensed food, and the bare essentials of existence, practically sank the *Little Willow* right there as we started upriver. I attached the ten horse kicker. I meant to use it as far up as Bettles and there send it back to Les. We couldn't afford to run a ten-horse kicker when we got beyond the gas stations.

With a scant three inches freeboard, we started out to buck the big Koyukuk. The large kicker attached to our square stern made our canvas canoe seem even smaller and more fragile than before; that kicker would soon take the back right out of our canoe from vibration!

The swift Koyukuk current laid hold of us and bore us backward downstream. The motor caught with a roar. Waves flew from the prow and a mighty wake spread behind us. Chunks of muddy drift shot by, but the shore line barely moved! For an hour the contest continued. We were faced with traveling ten miles of river drift to gain one-mile upstream. An hour's run took us only a mile above Hughes. Then the tank ran dry.

Before I could finish "gassing up," we had slid back to Hughes again. Foolishly, I flooded the motor, and in this way, jerking on the starting rope as fast as I could, I saw Hughes drift by and fade away as we rounded the bend below it. One hour's run and we were half a mile below town! The motor caught, again we fought our way upriver, only to have the motor die when it ran out of gas at practically the same spot. We repeated the same drift while I sweated on the starting rope again. A familiar sight on Alaskan rivers, this, in the summertime. I have seen many a fellow in the same spot.

There was the danger of being struck by the army of floating trees which rode down the flood in royal train and besides, we weren't getting anyplace.

We would just have to wait for the Koyukuk River to drop.

At Hughes I found Fred, one of the many natives in Alaska who are of part white blood, yet who are called "natives." He had a powerful inboard motor built into his heavy plank river boat. I agreed to furnish Fred with the gasoline and oil if he would tow us along with his party when the river dropped. This he was glad to do, for with most of our load stowed on his boat, he could tow us with ease.

The day Fred got ready to leave was a rainy one. He and I struggled, puffed, and slapped mosquitoes as we transferred a drum weighing four hundred pounds from Les's big barge to Fred's river boat. Then Fred opened up the supposed drum of gas. "Cylinder oil," he said, and I realized that after all that work, we had loaded the wrong drum. The mosquitoes got in more licks at us while we corrected our mistake and doggedly loaded the right barrel.

Fred's complete party was revealed to us when we stopped after ten hours' travel to stretch foot on land and cook supper. It consisted of Fred and his young wife—his third, since the first two had died—and two small infants we never did place, as Indians and Eskimos have a custom of passing their children around from one family to another. A young couple in their teens accompanied Fred's family, and had charge of one of these tots, a perfect baby doll of an Indian child; the young girl had the task of caring for this child, which had been wished off on her by relatives, no doubt. Her casual and neglectful treatment of the chubby little orphan caused it to wail often and loudly. Nobody interfered.

The young couple were honeymooning. They were not yet married but hoped to be. On the Koyukuk, where the bishop or the commissioner only gets by every year or two, marriage customs aim at convenience and practicality. The missionary women at Alatna had no powers to marry or bury although bury they must. When the chance offered this young couple would be legally married according to the laws of the Territory and the Church.

Muskrat season had just passed, and our crowd was flush with traders' goods at the moment. Most of the year meat and fish are the staff of life of these people, not bread. It is really a pity when bread does become the staff of life of any people, for bread lone lacks vitamins; hence the people fall ill, and their teeth and bones decay. Fish and game are actually more nutritious food. Now canned pears at seventy-five cents the can and Argentine corned beef at fifty cents, and endless gallons of black-brewed coffee with sugar and condensed milk, made up the meal. We were not invited to share in this hard-earned fare, and felt a little envious as we spread out our own modest sourdough pancakes and dried meat, picking wild onions from the riverbank for our own extra vitamins.

"Did you notice the shoes the bride is wearing?" asked Connie.

They were mail-order, white, high-heeled pumps. The bride wore them about the riverbank quite as though she had on hip boots. By the time we reached Alatna the heels had come off both of them, but this seemed to make little difference to her.

So, it was that we made our way back to Alatna some days later, traveling with the Indians.

The longest day of the year had already passed. We thought of this feverishly, for there was not a moment to waste. How would we live and be clothed in the new land beyond the timberline? This was our concern. As the sun turned south, we tried to get north, but seemed balked in our efforts. A day's run with the motor in our canoe above Alatna only proved that this part of the Koyukuk was too much for us to navigate. Here, in fact, the big river boats of the traders must often proceed by cable. We had attached the most powerful motor possible for the canoe's size, with the result that it came near to shaking the canoe to pieces, yet accomplished little against that mighty sweep. Slim, narrow, plank-built boats were capable of bucking this river to Bettles, where the Koyukuk branches and where we had hoped to "line" up the John River, but not our canvas canoe. Yet if we had used such a plank river boat, how could it have been portaged? We had thought of all this in planning for canvas. Or how could a plank boat be put into an airplane in pieces to fly?

Fly! That was it! While I was in Fairbanks, I had come pretty close to a new slant on our course, seeing it from the civilized perspective. We wanted to get to the arctic coast this summer. Maybe it would be best to get Wein Airlines to take us and our entire outfit over the hump to any place on the north slope watershed where a landing could be made. Of course, landing fields didn't exist, but how about landing on some broad river bar? Or on a lake, with floats?

We were ashamed to look our missionary friends in the eye when we came back to Alatna again because they must have thought this time that they were really rid of us. But there was clearly nothing we could do but have a plane come especially to Alatna for us a difficult assignment. We begged leave to set up our tent upon the mission lawn by the edge of the Koyukuk and keep our own house until the plane could come. This granted, in a trice we had pitched our tent and set about unpacking every item in the canoe, after sending out a radio telephone call by the half-Indian store owner there. Then came the removing of the skin of the canoe and 2000 screws to take it apart for its aerial trip. Two days later the canoe was a pile of slats and a bundle of canvas, while, living on early salmon, we were waiting, waiting. We were to wait at this spot almost a month more, or until mid-July, which was most of our traveling summer!

There is probably no one who has lived in Alaska who has not had the experience of being stuck at some outlandish place, waiting for an airplane that never comes. It was not until much later that the real story was made fully comprehensible to us. It shows what the airlines or any other utility is up against in northern pioneering, and to just what extent to date the airplane has "conquered the arctic."

Near July Fourth when the mail plane landed on the river bar at Alatna on its twice-monthly run, we had a chance to talk personally to one of the pilots, who came armed with information as his only defense against the attackers who swarmed around him. It would not be possible to make a landing with floats on the lake we had in mind just yet because Chandler Lake, high on the Arctic Divide, was still covered with ice. Had we only contacted the airlines three weeks ago a landing could have been made on this lake with skis, but this was the intermediate period. But just three weeks ago we ourselves had been frozen in on another point in the divide at the same time. Well, we would have to wait for the ice to melt in Chandler Lake then. How much did our outfit weigh? We had weighed and listed each item, including the canoe, all the gasoline we hoped to take to the Arctic Ocean, and ourselves, and after finding the amount to be 1400 pounds cut it down to 1050 pounds minimum, which left only 100 pounds of food for the whole next year's grub stake—and we were eating on that now. But 1050 pounds! The pilot clasped his head.

"My God, no float ship now in Alaska can get off the water with that!" The float ship was out.

We learned that small airplanes using pontoons, which a cording to the enthusiasts convert every arctic pond by summer into a natural landing area, can only carry a few pounds in them—and without a complete camping outfit in the arctic, you can't go anywhere. With a camping outfit you are perfectly safe there, but it is suicidal not to have one. Flying Fortresses make forced landings, and the crews, "rescued," are rushed to the hospital after two days of arctic life. Connie and I spent two years in the arctic and of course came out the same as usual because we were equipped to camp.

As a means of conveyance to a remote and uninhabited country where one expects to live, or possibly might be forced to live through some accident, the airplane is every bit as much of a problem when it comes to figuring your load capacity as the more primitive dog sled or motorized canoe; all of them eat their own weight and they eat more, of course, the larger and more expensive they are before they get well started. The dog sled served explorers not so long ago because it could find its subsistence along the way; the little canoe is not so bad because you can paddle it or sail it yourself by your own power in summer; an airplane is the worst problem of all if anything unexpected happens.

If we ever planned to be set down at Chandler Lake, we would have to make three charter trips to get ourselves and our load in there, which would take a small fortune. We could fly almost around the world on the regular air routes for what it costs at the present time to fly in the arctic part of our world, where even the fuel must be brought in by air, since there are no ground communications.

"What other place on the north side of the Brooks Range could a plane land, if not on water?" I asked. "A big plane with wheels that could take us and our year's outfit in one trip into that north country?" That was a big order, and I feared the answer.

The pilot explained that there was, in fact, one landing field on the "other side" just now in the process of being built; this place was a secret experimental naval oil-drilling camp not then shown on civilian maps. His pilot's map showed it to be on the lower Colville River. Its name was Umiat, not an Eskimo village there never had been an Eskimo village there but a modern arctic camp of white men, mushroomed up out of nothing since a few weeks ago. The Colville River! Flowing north of the timber line for a thousand miles into the Arctic Ocean, the Colville River has probably been seen by the number of white men which could be counted on the fingers of one hand and then usually by winter dog sled only, or by pilots from the air. You might say that a white man has never had a boat on it in summer. And summer is the whole life and essence of a river's existence. Not all of its course even has been definitely located on any map; only a few people know of its existence. Aside from a few men of the United States Coast and Geodetic Survey and the Geological Survey and a few pilots who have had cause to scratch their heads and wonder, there is nobody to know whether a thousand-mile-long river is placed in the right position on the maps or not. The white population of Alaska, dwelling along the southerly coasts, has never heard of it for the most part, although it is one of Alaska's largest rivers. Yes, we had dreamed of using the Colville for our highway down the north slope of the Arctic Divide. But the Colville is the kind of project which takes planning. We had lived a year near the edge of timber in hopes of getting the opportunity to venture beyond the timber the second year. This second year had at last come.

How would it be managed? "Well," said the pilot, "here's our trouble, see? We've got our big ship now up at Point Barrow and it's still on skis, so we can't land it down here yet." "Then we'll have to wait here until all the snow at Point Barrow melts?"

The pilot became indulgent. "Fellah," he said wearily, "you don't know what trouble fliers have. I'm not to blame for the snow at Point Barrow. The Bellanca will get on wheels and run to Bettles in a bit. It's too bad you kids couldn't make it in your canoe up the Koyukuk to Bettles, because what I'm wondering about now is how we'll get you and your canoe from here up to Bettles to where the Bellanca or the Boeing could reach you when it comes south. You know we couldn't bring those planes down here they're too big to try to land at Alatna with no field. I don't know just what we'll figure out for that. Some little plane like mine will first have to make several trips to shuttle your stuff to Bettles. Well, so long. I got to get over to the Bering Sea this evening before chow. But we'll get you out of here one of these days," he called on the run.

It resulted in a periodic shuttling of our load to Bettles bit by bit, by various pilots in small planes whenever they happened to be coming through our part of the world, until we ourselves went on the last shuttle.

It was a Sunday evening after festivities at the mission house and Connie had put on a dress and put wild primroses in her hair, when our airplane—the one that was actually to convey us to Bettles—roared abruptly over the house, shaking the dishes in the cupboard. "Airplane! Airplane!" came the shrill cries of the village children, who can hear a powerboat coming upriver thirty-six hours before it arrives and who can distinguish an airplane on the horizon from a bird or a speck. The dogs of the Indians lifted their muzzles to the sky in the familiar forest river wail. "Take the dress with you, Connie. You never can tell, you might want a dress sometime later on," I heard Miss Hill and Miss Kay saying, as Connie made for our tent on the run to don her trousers. Connie accepted the dress and stockings and threw them pell mell into the duffel sack. I believe the missionaries wanted to give us everything they owned!

The plane was coming down on the river bar below, and I had got one side of the tent down. But even with assistance from all sides it was forty minutes before we could convey everything into the mission boat, land the boat at the bar, unload the boat, and load the waiting airplane. Wedged in between boxes and duffel we sat in the cockpit, the three of us pilot, Connie, and I. Connie had our big iron skillet in her lap and it was full of grease and cooked salmon; at the last minute there was no time to dump it and the pilot was in a hurry.

The pilot grumbled. He didn't like it. We were loaded too heavily. We saw the anxious faces of the two lone missionary women as natives pushed the plane out of the gravel, to the accompaniment of loud racing of the motor. The pilot prepared to take off. For better or for worse, it was good-by to good friends on the lovely winding Koyukuk good-by to the forests and timber. We wondered.

Down the river bar we sped, dodging stumps and piles of drift, and just as it seemed he would run into the river, the pilot pulled her up and we were away. It was all part of the everyday business of a bush pilot in Alaska. Good-by! And we saw the scene under us that Alaskan pilots always see the faces below upturned to the sky.

4

The town of Bettles, the air traveler would note in his diary, lay just thirty minutes away. Yet we had been a month reaching it! The Navy was said to be building an immense airfield here; actually. the new project appeared under our wheels five miles further on, at a location called at that time Little Bettles.

Before us caterpillars and carryalls crawled over a gray muddy scar set down in the sea of arctic green. An excellent gravel runway, capable of accommodating the world's largest land planes, was being constructed. A group of tents and shacks flashed by as we came to a rolling stop by row on row of naval oil drums.

While Connie hurried to unpack our belongings from the plane and get them to the side of the field, I helped the pilot gas up his plane to go on. In many places this is done by chopping a hole in each five-gallon can with an ax and pouring tank did not suddenly get full when a can was upended, and the gasoline spill out all over the wings and fuselage with gas at seventy-five cents to a dollar a gallon.

"You going to wash her down with gas?" I asked. "Sure," he grinned. "Sig's got plenty of it."

The plane wouldn't start, and I flipped the prop while the pilot used the starter. The engine caught. The fellow wished us luck, and having promised that the Boeing would pick us up here tomorrow, he left.

"I hope this tomorrow has only twenty-four hours in it." We watched the plane sail off. It was nine o'clock at night and the pilot still had a five-hour run before he quit. Other people were waiting somewhere, stuck at some spot in Alaska, just as we had been.

We threw up our tent among the oil drums by the runway where heavy caterpillars rumbled all night long.

No one was in sight when we awoke on the next shift except a grease monkey greasing a "cat." I recalled the time an old northern man was telling us about his dogs and his cat and Connie had thought the cat was a pet and said, "Why my goodness, do you have a cat, too?" and was all ready to find it to pet it.

I walked over to the mechanic. "Hello, Bud," he called. I couldn't place him for a minute and he went on to say that we hadn't met but he knew we were up the Alatna River last winter and he and his wife had often wondered how we made out. He was a Kobuck from Alatna and his trap line was up the Henshaw River. We talked with the ease and familiarity that people who live in the far reaches of the arctic have with one another. He was an Eskimo who was also part Negro, part Hawaiian, and part Philippine. Asiatic strains are found in many of the natives of Alaska. This is due to imported cannery workers in the salmon industry in southern Alaska and to the whaling fleet which came to the Arctic Ocean in former days.

The fellow told me in a few minutes about the layout of this naval camp and how things were going. "Yes," he said, "the Boeing will be in today. Going to Umiat and back to Barrow, I hear." There were perhaps forty men working here at Little Bettles. We had heard that there were a great many more than that, but that's the way it turns out in these cases so often; usually the actual number is just a few, although of course anything approaching thirty or forty people of any kind all together is a tremendous crowd when you start thinking about any country north of the Yukon. The field here was under the supervision of the Navy Department but a private contractor was doing the job. His outfit was building a few hangars on the opposite side of the field, but as for living quarters, at present everyone lived in a tent camp over where the Koyukuk River splits up. This camp was connected to the runway by a path.

"Stop and see my wife. She gets lonely for someone to talk to," directed the arctic trapper as he turned back laconically to his machine and the wage of $400 a month which held him here for a short while.

The path to the camp quarters had been built upon a swamp in the wintertime. Now it was summer. The tent houses were connected with each other and to a cookshack by mats of sticks, odd logs of uneven lengths, and planks which sagged in the middle. Out of seemingly bottomless lakes of slime arose little islands of tin cans. The whole ground quivered like jelly under one's tread. Alongside the trail sat monstrous sleds in the mud, where they had been discarded till freeze-up the sleds of the modern arctic caterpillar train! They were much like railroad boxcars. It was by winter caravans that the heavy equipment had been hauled here across country when the ground was frozen, from the end of the railroad at Fairbanks. The camp had in this way been moved in and set up in very early spring for the summer's work. When swamps and lakes and rivers are frozen into iron the cat trains can travel almost at will over the arctic, pulling their big boxcars behind them. It was in the winter that Russia invaded Finland. Any northern country's offensive of the summer must be prepared in this way in the winter months before, and so it was with the construction of this Alaskan arctic airfield.

We noticed then that there was a white woman in camp. There she was, working to beat the dickens, and white, sure enough. She wore slacks and was middle-aged and she had a power washing machine set up on a system of boards and planks above the lake right beside the only building, the mess hall and cookshack, which she and her husband ran.

"Go say hello," I said to Connie, nudging her ahead; Connie did so, and I followed. But the washing machine made a great clatter and little conversation was possible because the woman seemed extremely busy. For some reason these camps which mushroom up always seem suspicious and resentful of an outsider at first. This is especially true with the women, when there are any. With their fresh foods flown from Fairbanks and their comparative luxuries, the people of the Alaska camps may be clannish, and they usually are hoping to make their stake and then get out of the country as soon as possible. But they are real workers!

We found out about dinner and then went on to chat with the native mechanic's wife and buxom Eskimoid daughters in their clapboard tent shack. One girl was lying ill with the earache. No doctor was to be had merely a little oil of cloves. Another teen-age sister had died in this house and had been buried a few weeks ago, we were casually informed. We were urged to have coffee and eat, but declined.

Interrupting our talk came the ring of a piece of grader blade suspended from a wire in front of the mess hall. The cook was beating out his dinner serenade with a rusty hammer. With cautious steps we skipped over the sagging planks of the swamp, entered the mess hall, and found a long clean room filled with eaters and with tables laden with food. Construction camp workers have real meals. Fried meats, potatoes of some sort, hot breads, pie, cake, canned fruits, and conserves are placed on the table regularly at each meal, including breakfast. The whole display was a picnic to us, although it did not occur to Connie until she was half through the meal that this was the first pork, or really the first domestic meat, she had eaten in a year and a half. The missionaries lived on things like home-canned caribou and salmon.

The conversation of the men was as much of a novelty to us as the meal was. We asked a fellow about this town of Umiat to which we were going. "It's a Seabee camp," he said

"just started up this season. Drilling for oil, I hear." "How many there?" We had heard all the way up to three thousand. "Oh, forty maybe. They come and go."

About here we became interested in an argument at the lower end of the table. "You can have it all north of Tulsa," one coarse-faced workman brayed as he tried to eat a quarter of a pie from the tin which he had squashed down upon his own plate still filled with mashed potatoes and gravy. The other fellow had a chance to speak as he succeeded in getting all but the crust into his mouth. "Oh, you never done more than pick cotton there, Okie."

The pie eater exploded. "Ah'm going back as soon as Ah can."

Leaving $2.50 under our plates, we suddenly scrambled, for just then the hum of a twin-motored plane came to my ear above the sound of the field machinery. The Boeing was landing on the runway as we reached the field. It was a Wein Airlines ship and reminded one of the airlines of the late '30s, a good buy for Alaska with all of its hazards.

Pilot, copilot, and a couple of the passengers helped load our things aboard. The native woman with her daughters stood by to see us off, and at the last moment pulled some extra bobby pins out of her hair and gave them to Connie because she knew that Connie was distressed about not being able to buy any with which to start the new wilderness year. With a last call from these friends, "Look out for the blizzards!" we were soon taxiing down the field, snapping our safety belts tight, and rushing forward for the take-off.

Once more Alaskan country slid beneath us as we banked, swerved, and then headed straight out up the John River for the divide.

A good deal has been written about the Alaska of the forest belt, which we were leaving; now we were going from the known to the unknown. Very little has been written in recent years about the land north of the timber on our continent. For myself, my impressions of it were vague. In grade school my geography books had laid down a definite place on earth called the "tree line." I had understood that tall mountains have a tree line and the earth likewise. This is determined by the "terrible cold." Surely now we would see the tree line running along here somewhere, we thought. Yet spruce forest continued to grow in patches here and there in the sheltered places of the mountains, while we were over a hundred miles north of the Arctic Circle. When I later learned that there are, in fact, forests on the upper parts of most of the larger rivers which flow into the Arctic Ocean, and that in some places spruce timber runs right up to within a few miles of the Arctic Ocean itself, while I knew that the Aleutian Islands two thousand miles to the south are barren, I was confused but not dismayed. Clearly then, cold does not have everything to do with the dispersal of timber. The coldest temperatures on this continent are recorded in its interior in the Yukon Territory, which is heavily timbered. I do not pretend to know anything about tree dispersal, but owing to the presence of the Arctic Ocean Connie and I would not encounter this year colder temperatures on the northernmost points of land of this continent than we had already experienced.

Bands of white, bighorn Dall sheep fell under the plane's shadow as we passed over their highland domain. The highest altitude of the Brooks Range is ten thousand feet. A snow storm hid the valley floor; then presently we emerged in sunlight over the most idyllically peaceful green pastures I had ever seen. As far as the eye could see there lay nothing but gently rolling, grass-covered mountain meadows. Their rounded domes spoke of age; the abundance of their verdure spoke of fertile soil. Yet probably no one will ever farm the world's last great open prairies which roll around our globe in the high latitudes.

Here is a prairie hunter's dream come true. Here roam the

occasional Barren Grounds' grizzly bear and the moose although most people, even woodsmen of Alaska, do not dream that the moose emerges from the most far northern coniferous forests to roam three hundred miles beyond the last tree. Here are millions of nesting waterfowl by summer, breeding in numbers as great as Canada's own. We have no inventory yet and are just beginning to realize what Alaska has. We don't know what herds of caribou are shared between Alaska and Canada on these plains. There is no fence to stop them and they are wandering animals. Yet few are the white men living who have ever seen the caribou, whose herds roam these great pastures very much as they always have.

As our airplane passed on at 180 miles an hour, from the spruce-covered drainage basin of the Koyukuk and Yukon Rivers to the scattered spruce and willow pockets of the Brooks Range, the Brooks Range itself had given way at some indeterminate point to this true prairie beyond the timber. The Brooks Range leans to the north. It gradually changes into what geographers have named broadly the Arctic Plateaus. These plateaus are on slightly different levels and are separated from each other by what is generally agreed to be ten major rivers flowing at regular intervals of about forty miles apart, down the north front of Alaska into the Arctic Ocean. According to the explorer Leffingwell (1919) these rivers are "reported to head against the Yukon drainage" and on the maps are named the Turner, Hulahula, Sadlerochit, Canning, Sagavanirktok, Aichillik, Jago, Okpilak, Shaviovik and the Kuparuk of which more later. Because they have Eskimo names, many of these rivers are spelled on each map you will see in a different way to this day. The big Colville, the eleventh river, was the one we were going down. After they wind through the Arctic Plateaus, the rivers enter the Arctic Coastal Plain, and finally the sea.

The quiet open spaces beneath our airplane were dappled in sun and shadow. Little blue lakes and potholes of all shapes and sizes dotted this prairie, which some people have called tundra or Barren Grounds. These are words which Connie and I do not take too seriously. We do not use them because they call up false impressions. The Barrens are not barren; the tundra is far from desolate. to us who have come to know and love prairie life. Most naturalists have always preferred to call this land prairie.

For two hours we traveled. Smoke could be seen streaming upward from some pin point on the dappled green plain before us, marking the presence of man beneath this curving sky of the boundless prairie. Before we drew closer, already gradually losing our altitude, we knew that this must be Umiat. Now a line of dark green on the dim sea below the nose of the Boeing marked the wandering course of the thousand-mile-long timber less Colville, or at least a part of it the unknown river which we had thought for so long to see, a big river as little known to civilized man as when Columbus landed. The dark green would be willows growing along it.

Umiat lay on the lower Colville; there was no landing field yet completed, but landing could be made with the big Boeing on the exposed river bar after the receding of the Colville's spring floods. The floods had receded just a week before this time, so that for this reason again we could not have made a contact here to start our canoe voyage down to the Arctic Ocean any sooner.

Swinging low over the river, we banked steeply. The Colville was no longer a ribbon, some distant dream. It was a real river and it looked mighty big. Yet a person couldn't tell how big right off because there were no trees or other basis for comparison by which the passenger could accurately gauge the river's breadth. No people or dwellings were visible. There seemed to be an embankment or cliff following one side of the river when we got close.

"I see caribou tracks in the sand there below," I told Connie, but she was too dizzy to look as we banked. Those tracks came up at me for an instant just as clear as type. "There is food here anyway!" was what I thought, with my mind on the hazardous year ahead.

Now we flashed by a wind sock and a conical tent of army drab about the size of the Indian tepee of American folk lore. That single tent, when you saw it, and that one wind sock flapping in the breeze looked pretty lonely somehow. Our wheels touched gravel; we rolled to a stop.

Outside the airplane windows, with their olive-green mosquito head nets pulled down, as in the jungle pictures, stood two lone Seabees the people.

Connie awaits the Boeing at Little Bettles airstrip

The Boeing arrives at Umiat

5

It had taken us but little over two hours to come by airplane across the Arctic Divide. By canoe it would have taken us two years.

As the motors of the Boeing died, we all leaned back and stretched. Everything was very still, after the sudden ceasing of motion and vibration. We yawned and popped our ears, we looked at the two Seabees standing out there and they looked back. The pilot flung open the door. There were things for Umiat to unload. Everything here, even the men, came by air, and the base was entirely air serviced aside from a couple of caterpillar trains in winter. Then the Point Barrow passengers and we ourselves became fully aware of our environment. For no sooner had the big motors died than a strange, ominous black cloud was seen rising up under the wheels and wings of the plane and enveloping it. Mosquitoes! Billions of them!

Opening the airplane's door, we stepped out into a world of a billion wings. The mosquitoes had not been so bad on the Koyukuk; we were used to them. These here were the largest mosquitoes we thought we had ever seen. With some difficulty we found our head nets and got them on. The other passengers, who were men in ordinary business suits and who had no head nets with them, began clapping the mosquitoes which poured into the plane, and the door was slammed shut. With all haste we were unloaded, wished well on our way, and the business being transacted, the Boeing took off and was gone. Just like that.

We looked around. There was everything we owned laid out on the beach in neat piles which Connie had already covered with our tent. There were the bundles of slats which were the *Little Willow*. Had we forgotten any of the bundles or were parts missing? Could we ever get her together again, this homemade canoe of ours which was not a canoe at all at the present time, but only an idea? Could we really go down to the Arctic Ocean on the mythical Colville, which, so far as we were concerned, was as yet only an idea too?

The complete camp outfit carried by the canoe consisted of:

1 miner's shovel
1 small, homemade, sheet-iron stove
1 wall tent, 8' x 10', with 3-foot walls
1 Johnson 1½-horsepower outboard motor
1 5½-foot canoe paddle 1 6-foot light oar
1 Model 12 Winchester 12-gauge pump shotgun 2 .30-30 Winchester carbines
1 Remington .2 2 bolt action rifle
1 .22 Colt Woodsman pistol
1 Three-Star Woods Arctic Sleeping Bag
1 caribou fur blanket and two wool blankets
3 small stewpans
2 pie plates, spoons and forks
1 stainless-steel mixing bowl and big spoon
1 fish net, 2½-inch mesh, 3 feet deep, 30 feet long (gill net)
About 200 rounds ammunition for each arm
About 100 pounds dried and condensed foods, mainly flour, sugar, and home-dried meat'
About 40 gallons gasoline and 3 gallons cylinder oil
1 small tool kit for the motor
1 water bucket, 2½-gallon capacity
2 axes, 2½ size
Our few clothes and a camera Zeiss Contax, 35 mm.
2 pairs of snowshoes (Indian made)
1 meat grinder
1 DDT spray gun

The load was balanced m the canoe with the heaviest items placed in the middle, while we sat in back together. The canoe rode level for going downstream.

We looked around, as I say, and the place looked like the end of the earth. We weren't quite at home here yet, but seeing a familiar species of gull from the North Pacific flying overhead and noticing that the grass and the sky and a lot of old friends of that sort were with us even here, we surmised that we would feel at home presently.

For years we had thought about seeing this most inaccessible of all rivers, down which a canoe ride would be, in all events, a one-way ticket. Well, we had plenty of time; we could spend a year or several years in this country if we liked it. Of course, it would take a year anyway to get out. It was thanks to the new camp at Umiat that we were here. I felt like a fellow who has won an elephant in a raffle.

As for the two Seabees, they stood looking unbelievingly at us, while a light rain commenced to fall. We stepped up to them, offered our hands from out our canvas gloves for one moment, and all introduced ourselves, but didn't raise our head nets. We told them we were going down to the Arctic Ocean to do some canoeing this summer, and said we would begin reconstruction of our canoe at this spot if there were no objections. Could we erect our tent here?

"Why yes, of course," was the open-mouthed reply, "but why not use ours? "We don't sleep in it. It's just for plane cargo." Accepting the offer, we found the drab-colored conical tepee completely mosquito-proofed with the aid of the new war-developed DDT bombs.

Connie and I commenced to untie the canoe slats from their bundles as the two fellows watched. There were around forty men connected with the camp, all told, inclusive of some parties of surveyors and geologists out scouting in the vicinity; these two men had come with the first original cat train. Much about them was clear from their silence that they were seasoned or had been out for a long time. They asked us almost no questions and did not chatter. I told them it wasn't so awfully long ago that I too was in the service. The Seabees watched with absorbed curiosity as we began work. Then one of them said: "Have you got an extra screw driver? I'll help." Soon we were all companionably working on the canoe. We thought it was daytime but that must have actually been a midnight lunch which our new friends presently brought out to us from the main camp steak, and a giant carton of fresh-frozen peas!

Our tent beside the gravelly river bar which had been smoothed bulldozers and marked out by red flags was equipped with a

Walkie-Talkie field radio telephone which the boys said to use to notify camp if we wanted anything. We used it on one occasion to notify camp that a plane had just come in which had been unable to make contact with headquarters due to a temporary faultiness in radio. The pilot was Sig Wein, the owner of Wein Airlines. His run frequently took him to Umiat between Point Barrow and Fairbanks and he wanted to see us. His question was, did we want him to look for us, and just when should he start looking, in case we didn't turn up from this Colville River and Arctic Ocean canoe trip?

This famous Alaskan flier has searched for many a missing person. He has been known to have every plane out and spare no personal expense in matters pertaining to rescue. An old Alaskan custom, this can mean a lot. Much impressed with Sig's rescue offer, we told him no. we felt that persons who ventured along the arctic coast would have to take care of themselves entirely because there would be no way for them to notify the world if rescue were needed. Somebody will ask at this point why we didn't take a radio. We couldn't take one. Equipment which would reach far enough to be of any use weighs too much to lug in a fourteen-foot canoe. Even the usual small airplane radio, like the Walkie-Talkie, is of use only if there is another station within a radius of fifteen or twenty miles and in the arctic you are dealing with distances of hundreds of miles.

By the time a searching party could organize, it would be too late for a rescue in our case, we thought. Searching parties are an extremely expensive and inconvenient burden to impose upon the shoulders of other people; if one has the selfishness to put himself into a foolish position, he must take the full responsibility himself and should not risk other lives needlessly. Besides, as we told Sig, we were quite used to being grounded and on our own all the time anyway; the arctic was our natural habitat, we had been existing this way for some time already, and we had not a doubt in the world but that we would be perfectly all right anyplace so long as we had our rifles and fish nets and camping equipment with us. Home is where you make it, after all. We were quite confident that canoeing in the Arctic Ocean would come naturally after we got the hang of it; our reasons for this will be given in some detail later. We planned, then, to spend the winter somewhere along the arctic coast and hence could be expected to have no communications during the year. Our final destination was Aklavik, Canada, to the eastward, which we expected to reach the following summer.

No airplanes in Alaska fly east of Point Barrow along the arctic coast, Sig told us definitely, so that we might be forewarned of what we were doing. Sig ran the only private airline to Point Barrow, Alaska, which is Uncle Sam's farther most point of land and most remote outpost. He probably knew more about the arctic coast line than any other white person now in Alaska but that, he regretted, wasn't much. Only on two occasions in history that he knew of, aside from the former flight by Sir Hubert Wilkins, polar explorer, had an airplane of any kind flown eastward from Point Barrow, and these two flights were of his own planes. There was nothing to the east of Point Barrow but a few Eskimos. Sig didn't know how many there were, but he said we should expect to find Eskimos encamped along the shore this summer, scattered here and there, he thought, but usually they spoke no English at all; and as for white men, them was not a single white man on the north coast of Alaska or in a thousand miles of undulating arctic coastline today, as a canoeist would see it.

"But how about traders? Aren't there some traders up there?" we asked. Genial Sig dispelled this idea with a sweep of the hand. There used to be traders, he said. We knew ourselves from reading the old books that the Arctic Ocean used to be fairly bustling with explorers and whaling ships and trading enterprises, but all our information gleaned from the public libraries was pretty old. Even talking with people in the cities of Alaska, we couldn't learn anything, because most of them were newcomers just like ourselves. We had imagined living the coming winter at, well who knows? Herschel Island in Canadian waters over east a ways, if we got that far this season. We believed that we would find an Eskimo community there, perhaps even missionaries and numbers of Canadian officials. That was all wrong. The arctic was not what it had been twenty-five years ago. It was almost depopulated. To our dismay we learned that there was nobody on Herschel Island or in fact in this part of the arctic in either Alaska or Canada. It was hard to tell exactly what a traveler would find now, since so many Eskimos had been attracted to Point Barrow to settle down near the trader, school, and church; likewise, many Eskimos near the border of Alaska and Canada, who had not been drawn to Barrow in Alaska, had been drawn far over into the Canadian side to reside at Aklavik, Canada's greatest arctic outpost, not on the Arctic Ocean at all but actually some sixty miles inland up the delta of the Mackenzie River in the forest area.

We would have to find Eskimos, and find them soon, this summer, to learn to live on the north coast when we got there. As to food, we were used to hunting but still it was a little different here, and we would have to learn how well game flourished in a local area by experience with it. But clothing and fuel were our biggest problems. Our little sheet-iron camp stove set up on the beach at Umiat burned twigs hardly larger than a pencil limber, wretched willow roots. Would the bushes and willows get smaller still as one progressed down the river to the ocean front? One assumed they would. But we counted on finding driftwood there.

The fuel situation on the timber less Colville River and its kind is a major reason why the white man has scarcely yet set foot in Eskimo land. The explorers had their special kerosene burning primus stoves, but we hadn't been able to get hold of anything like that. The whalers had had their ships to live on, of course, while we would have to find materials somehow out of which to build our own winter's home. We were hastening into this country by summer and must solve our fuel situation before winter came. So, reasons the white man. But other human beings are living here all the time, and they don't even seem to have to worry.

Again, we were going down to the arctic coast without the right clothing. Last year in the timber belt we had got along with our present white-man woolens, what with a good log cabin and a big drum heater inside it and plenty of fuel for the chopping. But this year we must find Eskimos to make us the real Eskimo clothing or contrive it of caribou skins ourselves, for we had not been able to obtain it from forest Indians or in any other way. In fact, we had lived several years in Alaska and had never seen fur clothing. It is generally not obtainable for the public. Yet on these prairies where there is nothing to break the winds, a person just can't live in white man's clothing alone in winter, unless it is something of special arctic design, insulated with waterfowl down or whatnot. We had only a few weeks of grace, we knew, to solve these problems of existence in a land which was strange to us, but we trusted that they would be solved. One experience which we had always longed for was to actually wear a real suit of Eskimo fur clothing and see what that was like. Sig and we and a young pilot he had with him just over from South China stood talking thus on the landing bar of the Colville River and Sig had on a decorative squirrel parka, having just come from the north coast, and the rest of us were in fabric jackets and mosquito head nets. Sig had seen the lower reaches of the Colville from Umiat down, by air, and reported no waterfalls in the river, at any rate. We laughed. "Well, got to get going. I'll be seeing you sometime then."

"Thanks for everything."

The rest of the canoe went together fast. The canvas was on and the paint was on as far as it would go that is, we didn't have quite enough paint to cover the second outside canvas we had added as an afterthought, so that a streak some six inches wide was left unpainted along one side. The extra layer of canvas was a kind of insurance toward ocean navigation.

Meantime the Seabee camp telephoned us to come to the mess hall for dinner and meet everybody. The camp had already talked to Connie over the Walkie-Talkie and informed her that they much desired her presence at dinner.

The bus which came by for us was a D-8 Caterpillar. It pulled a carryall, inside the cab of which three of us crowded, while perhaps fifteen sat on the top or hung onto the sides. The road was anywhere that the cat could navigate. At times the tracks were submerged in soupy mud. Rivers of water were pushed ahead of us as we backed and bucked and charged in several gears. Only the frozen subsoil at a certain depth seemed to keep us from sinking altogether as we rolled over the prairie, crushing earth and wildflowers.

"How come they build an airfield in a swamp?" I yelled conversationally.

"Oh, the Navy likes to be near water, you know," the kid driver laughed back in a high falsetto above the noise.

A group of prefabricated huts lined a muddy street. There were a couple of radio towers. The men were dirty and had long beards up to four inches in length, many of them having just been transferred directly here from a previous hitch in the Aleutians. They dressed like any contract workers and no sign of rank or military insignia was to be seen. We never did know who was in charge at Umiat but supposed he was there. Mostly the men were older, from thirty to forty years of age; they had been carefully picked from the ranks of skilled labor.

The oil rig where the drilling was to be done was six miles from camp and for this reason, we never saw it. They had not yet begun to get oil at this time and there was nothing to see except what could be found on the map: an area of 30,000 square miles dotted off, and which has been marked since 1926 as "Naval Petroleum Reserve."

We were led to the hospital hut where we washed up with hot water and soap. By the time we entered the mess hall it was already packed to capacity with eating men. We stood at the end of the line with our friends, and our plates, which were tin trays with depressions in them for the segregation of the different kinds of food, were filled. The cook, a 240-pounder, scrubbed and naked to the waist, and himself bristling with a black set of whiskers out of which gleamed merry cheeks, was a good one. It was the same kind of chow generally that you would get in the United States Navy in any part of the world.

After dinner we talked in the mess hall. Asked what they thought about the country here the men were divided as to their opinion of it, but there was one thing they were unanimous on: that they wished to go home. Some expressed a willingness to come back as contract workers if they could do so of their own volition and get paid for it; it seemed as though the termination of the war would find private contractors developing the naval arctic oil fields when they were developed. Under the men's discontent at this time, of course, was the longing of United States soldiers everywhere for the homes they had left behind, some of them as long as three or four years ago.

Almost every man had some little present for us, it seemed, when we left: candy bars, reading matter, and such things. Our contribution was a dozen fresh eggs which came along on the Boeing with us, which, when we realized the men had eaten only powdered eggs for months, we offered just to set the camp wild. How they divided that dozen eggs among forty men I cannot attempt to guess.

I had asked first and last if anybody here had ever seen anything of the Colville River by boat, and always got the same answer: No.

"No, a party of our geologists thought they might go down from here this spring and try to make it to Point Barrow when they hit the ocean. That was the trouble. They couldn't have got back. Then the water of the Colville looked too rough for them," they said.

"We didn't expect the Colville to be a swift river," said Connie. "Why, we're used to mountain rivers. But this is prairie. According to my calculations, the Colville should have a slow current."

"Well, they say it's swift, you know. Pretty fast run-off. You should have been here and seen it a few weeks ago."

Later that summer naval geologists did go down the river from Umiat, we understand, in a small boat, as far as the Anaktuvuk junction anyway. They were serviced by airplane.

Originally there was Brooks, who first recognized, with his party of American and Canadian geologists in 1916, that the Brooks Range, or Arctic Mountain System, as he called it then, was a separate system from the Rockies; and there was Ernest de K. Leffingwell, whose map of the north coast of Alaska still remains our standard authority today of this region: men like these know of the Colville or mention it conspicuously in their works. Some men of the Smith expedition out from Washington, D.C., in 1924 wintered on the Arctic Divide and canoed with Peterborough canoes down one of the branches of the Colville one summer.

Connie and I started down the Colville in 1945 living on cans of pressed chicken, chocolate nut bars, and fresh-frozen green peas. Our real grubstake was along too, of course some empty gasoline cans which we had boiled out and filled with all our flour and sugar to protect these items from dampness or contamination resulting from possible capsize. Then we had tea and some sacks of dried caribou meat, and a bucket of moose tallow: a person can live on this fare for weeks if he has to with no apparent decline in health, inasmuch as home-dried meat seems to lose vitamins only very slowly. It was a wonderful lark going down that river in the golden summertime, one of those experiences which are unforgettable. Yet we are conscious of the fact that we left four fifths of the great river above, still to be seen by someone else more energetic than we, perhaps several years hence.

It was the Colville River which carried us to the Eskimo coast east of Point Barrow. No word had come out of this land for a quarter of a century.

The Seabees building Umiat, July 1945

We set off down the little known Colville River

# PART TWO

The Colville River

Mathew and his wife

Mathew's grown children

1

The only way to see the arctic part of our world at the present time is to have a private airplane or go by the rivers to the ocean in your own canoe. Explorers up to now have expected to live more or less off the country by hunting and fishing, and if they failed to do so, it meant the loss of life itself. Connie and I were having our first experience with the real treeless arctic, but we trusted that we, or probably anybody, could keep alive with a background of a good deal of general outdoors experience.

Often, we had discussed what the Colville River was like. Would it be a deep sluggish "tundra river" and look kind of like the Mississippi? Connie was sure it would be broad and muddy, and she had settled her mind long ago to this vision of it. But from the air as we first approached the Colville, I had said: "Well, I don't know. I see outcroppings of rocks here and there. I rather think we'll find ourselves camping on gravel river bars, and maybe no mud at all. Maybe the bottom of the river will be solid bedrock."

As we pushed out from the Umiat shore in our loaded canoe, Connie and I were given the answers to some of the questions about the Colville River right there. The river bed was lined with smooth rounded rocks, ranging from the size of a baseball on up! The water, to our surprise, was clear as a cat's eye: it was to be a swift river then, with at least some rapids. It was to be a beautiful river, too.

From where we had put our canoe together on shore, we could

see a big riffle stretching across the river about half a mile below town. As we neared this riffle, we weren't prepared for the sudden swift rise of the bottom beneath. The current kept trying to pull us to the right side where the river rushed through some big rocks, sending up spray, but we didn't want to go through there! The whole river shallowed at the riffle to what was possibly only four inches all the way across, so I retreated from this with the motor.

There was a place here where the river split and a small, insignificant channel cut through a spillway right under the bluff. Near the cut bank of a river is usually to be found the deepest channel, although one must be on guard for enormous boulders which have bounded down in ages past and lodged there from the bluff above. This channel, although not over ten feet wide, was very deep. The big riffle damming the river forced the rest of the water through here at a tricky pace. I kept the kicker barely running and in this way, we put on what brakes we could to our forward speed.

For all its wayward channels the Colville was a big river, carrying a good deal of water in it, and it would get progressively bigger and more navigable as it neared the ocean. Because the country was so flat, the river sprawled out, splitting into many divisions, so that though a person didn't know which channel to take, he had to make up his mind fast.

There were no trees, but willows growing up to twelve feet tall were along the watercourse to begin with. Our canoe had been named for the willow, symbol of life in arctic lands; it is a most hardy plant and might be seen growing even at the North Pole were there land at that spot. All arctic islands probably possess the willow if nothing else. Our canoe with us in it was destined to explore the land of the little willow, the appropriateness of whose symbol was now to be seen in creeping ground willows of a different leafage from that to which even we were used. These willows sprang crookedly from the soil. Their appearance reminded us of green dwarfed apple trees or perhaps some exotic tropical thorn bush. One notices carefully a feature like the growth of willows in a land where all other distinguishing characteristics are singularly absent.

The arctic in places during the summertime looks and is strangely tropical. First and last, I suppose the traveler would remember the mosquitoes on this arctic river in summer. Yet we find that we remember them only remotely because we took them for granted; they were merely one of the things you expect, if you know anything about the arctic at all to begin with. We were interested in other things. The two things which impressed us greatly about the Colville River, which make it different from all other rivers we have ever seen, were the peculiar high bluffs or headlands which followed. Neither of these could a person ever forget who has seen this river.

To describe the bluffs first. The point where we set sail down the arctic slope at Umiat began in the Arctic Plateaus. The plateau on which we journeyed is eighty miles wide at the Colville. In other words, the Brooks Range at this point sets back just eighty miles by air from the Arctic Coastal Plain. The rivers which cut through these plateaus are evenly spaced as they descend, and one of the interesting features about them is that they are sunk below the level of the plateaus so that from a quarter of a mile distant a pedestrian would have no hint of their existence or that a large river flowed there: they are hidden from the gaze. At least one of these rivers has cut into the plateau a thousand feet below the prairie's surface. The Colville behaves similarly, so that its western bluffs stand three hundred to four hundred feet below the earth's level. At first, we thought these bluffs were only local, but they marched off and then came back again to the present course of the river and so followed along with us for a hundred miles of the river's squirming travel, falling off one by one, romantically, toward the sea. The river bed soon grew to be from a mile to three miles wide and the romantic bluffs in the distance took on the rose, maize, and blue of prairie land.

It was as if the whole land suddenly came to a big step and dropped these four hundred feet, only to continue on as before at the lower level. The Colville River marked the dividing line between the elevations of different plateaus. In the shade of the cliffs on our left hand lay exposed strata of eternal ice, while colored spots of yellow, magenta, and blue were wildflowers overhanging from above. On our right hand lay sand dunes carved by wind and water and rolling grassy prairie as far as the eye could see. On this side, broad bands of color stretched out to the horizon in a flower-strewn featureless sameness everywhere. Aside from the eternal ice, under the bluffs into which the river cut, there was no snow, for summer comes even earlier to prairie than to forested mountain hundreds of miles to the south.

Our Summer with the Eskimos

It is very easy for an inexperienced person to become lost in such prairie country if he strays but a few miles from camp. The Colville bluffs from the one side served as the river's identification for fifty miles, but up on top of the bluffs themselves the prairie on that side of the river rolled on to a seemingly endless horizon. This is the kind of country that calls for the use of a compass and some knowledge of navigation before one starts on a hike.

We hadn't traveled very far on the river before we were hungry. There, on a smoothly polished gravel bar as large as ten city blocks, lay a big shaggy lump of peat left by the last flood. Connie held up a jar of cheese spread and a loaf of fresh bread and waved them at me. I nodded, and we pulled into a convenient eddy at the side of the bar. The peat looked like possible fuel, and this sunbaked river bar, surrounded by several hundred yards of moving water on every side, should be a good bet in mosquito country.

Not so! Even as we landed the mosquitoes could be seen as black specks covering the evenly laid rocks and crawling from behind them, ready to launch themselves. They stayed on the lee side of the rocks because they were clinging against a slight ground breeze, but it looked like a planned ambush. There was the lump of dry peat lying like a prostrate brown bear upon the gravel. I laid a match to it and a spurt of flame shot over the inert mass; then it lay smoldering away. The peat wasn't suitable fuel for cooking, but it made a fine smudge! We could sit in the smoke and eat our cold food. Connie and I take no coffee in our exploring and it was fortunate for us that we had long been used to content ourselves with water, for here was one of the many situations where the average picnicker or camper could have made himself very miserable if he was determined to brew his cup of coffee and then tried to strain the bugs out of it as he drank.

It is much better to give up one's pet habits and keep things simple. Why make them complicated?

Sitting with our backs bathed in smoke, we found the air about us to be black with the frail flimsy forms of the mosquitoes, tapping our poplin jackets lightly, like rain, as we ate. We were able to pull our mosquito head nets up to get in a few hurried bites, but it was not a leisurely meal. Trying to turn around and face the smoke, we put our faces almost into the fire, but our tormentors could take it better than we! Soon we were just like smoked sausages. When a person ventures into the inland summer arctic, the mosquitoes make a grand jubilee of this event which one supposes must be momentous in their otherwise dull existence.

Since we had had dealings with their kind before, we knew that the best way to get along is to just live in one's nets and forget them head net by day, bed net by night. The mosquitoes in this part of the world can make life miserable, even dangerous. It is not pleasant seeing the world from behind veils, but you must learn to live with them. People who smoke are handicapped and we didn't smoke. Many of the Seabees, driving their caterpillars through the mosquito clouds, persisted in burning a hole in their head nets from smoking their cigarettes with the net on. The mosquitoes poured in and the men went nearly mad.

Connie touched my shoulder with a gloved hand and pointed to the opposite shore of the river, beneath the cliffs. "Bull caribou," I told her as a gray form drank from the river across from us. The caribou stood watching us for several minutes; then he turned and speeded along upriver, looking for a gully between the cliffs. Soon we saw him clear up on top, like a little antlered ant, still trying to decide what we were.

"You can't tell if it's day or night," remarked Connie. I looked at my watch.

"It's eight o'clock at night," I told her, "and we've been traveling all day."

It may seem queer, but unless you resort to the compass or are sure of your direction, you cannot tell right off by the position of the sun circling the horizon whether it is 8 A.M. or 8 P.M. The irregularity of the hours you keep partly accounts for this.

"Let's travel until midnight," we decided. It was beautiful traveling weather. Surprises and delights rounded every bend.

Connie was grieved to be forced back from flower groves by the hordes of insects which inhabited these deceiving places. Each rebuff turned us again to the middle of the strange river which hurried us ever onward irretrievably from our last civilization.

Connie could certainly say she was the first white woman ever to have looked on this river. She was daily making her own discoveries and together we conferred.

"Look, squirrel tracks on the bank!" What's this? Squirrels north of timber line? No, we made a wrong guess from Connie's first "squirrel" tracks, and presently came to recognize instead that we had discovered Parry's spermophile. His other name is parka squirrel, or sik-rik, as the Eskimos call him, a rodent living in colonies, similar to the Kansas prairie dog. Some geologists, observing the countless thousands of meaningless knolls of a two-foot elevation which dot the great northern prairies, have attempted to evolve elaborate theories to account for them. Since the issue is still undecided, we would guess that the parka squirrels simply make the knolls. Just as the beavers have played an important role in the economy of the timber country to the southward, even adapting to their own needs by controlling erosion there, so the countless generations of parka squirrels stretching back into the beginnings of time have had to do with the peculiar conformations of probably a good share of the arctic prairie. Ahead of the canoe's bow the bluffs of the Colville marched into the hazy distance. We fairly boiled through turns around these bluffs at times. In the river's battle with the bluffs it was plain to be seen that the latter were losing every day. From time to time small landslides let go above and came crashing down into the water. Puffs of smoke trailing up from them could be seen both before and behind, as the current swung our canoe down along the tall columns. Dust of several of these miniature slides hung in the air along the miles of battlefront as we passed.

    The big river would stretch out over a vast gravel fault, only to shift its full power into a narrow channel and send it hurtling against its foe, the bluffs. We were obliged to follow it in its efforts. From some sandstone pinnacle standing above, some high escarpment, whose loose shale had thus far defied the forces of avalanche, we were dived upon by a hunting hawk or falcon. Such a bird would descend at each quarter of a mile from its nest to make mock attacks upon us. Hurtling from its nest filled with downy young, it screamed thrillingly.

    Rounding a curve, we surprised a flock of about three hundred Canada geese. They were hobbling, flightless at this season, along the barren shore. With the smoothness of a spreading tide they fled over the uneven stones as we approached, the legs of the little fellows twinkling faster than the eye could follow. Geese can run as soon as they are hatched from the shell; the long running strides of a man over the same ground are hard put·to it to overtake those twinkling little legs with their three-inch steps!

    Here was an unusual opportunity for close-up pictures. We did not have a movie camera, unfortunately, and were not equipped to manage it; we did not have telephoto lenses for photographing game. What we could get during this trip in the arctic were colored slides of places never photographed before, taken with a very fine lens. As luck would have it now, the geese had not been driven a quarter of a mile as we motored down the current when there appeared the immediate danger of the whole flock being pinned in beside us by the high rising bluffs. The cliff here stepped nearer the water. Accelerating the motor, I put the canoe right in close. Some geese made for the water and dove as we shot past.

The rest began to pour in a herd up a steep gully in the cliffs. Some fell over backwards. As the hundreds began to climb the bluff we were absorbed with their problem and did not note our own.

Abruptly, without warning, the whole river swung powerfully into the bluffs on a turn. The sand cliffs leaned out almost overhead; yes, some forty feet of the river's breadth actually ran into a yawning hole under the cliff, and we might be pulled into it but for a strong motor! "Never mind the geese!" Connie yelled. "Looks bad ahead. We better tend to business." It was all the little motor could do to pull us out of that one. The cliff face, with its dirty ice strata showing near the water line and its overhanging tons of dripping earth, flashed by, and the last of the geese were cut from sight.

"How many pictures did you get, Connie?"

"None! Oh! There were so many geese in every direction. I couldn't focus because it happened so quickly, and I couldn't decide what picture to take!"

We had hardly passed the geese and the undercut bluff when, the river having squirmed gently enough out onto the plain again, and the cliffs receding, a large bull caribou was seen prancing along the sand dunes on our right hand as though following our canoe. Racing to a point below, he beat us there and stood waiting, pawing and throwing dust on his back. He made you think of the wild stallions of the old West and a few today, still roaming over Utah. The general topography of the Arctic Plateaus in summer gives the appearance with their caribou! of badlands or desert lands.

This was not the rutting season of the caribou. What was this commotion all about? The bull stood there with a rack of knobby antlers three feet tall and in the velvet, rocking from side to side. As we were two hundred yards out in the river, he may have run to meet us in the belief that we were other caribou you might say, as a result of the herd instinct. This, I believe, was the answer to this peculiar case, for on these prairies in winter I subsequently saw animals do just this. While the herds are split up into just a few individuals in summer, the caribou in winter congregate in great bands.

Kicking his heels into the air and bucking as he ran, the frisky caribou took off again. We lost the wild fellow from view behind the willow fringe, but a mile below, there he was waiting for us on a point once more, having taken the pains to swim a hundred-yard channel to get there.

"That caribou's crazy," said Connie.

"I don't know," I told her, "but if he gets much further ahead of us, he'll get our scent.':

As he galloped inland once more, we could see his heavy antler rack swaying over the brush tops; presently, back he came, jumped into the river, and swam the next side channel. Emerging below, a hundred yards from us where the river turned, he shook himself like a dog and was apparently at once made dry from this icy plunge. Suddenly I knew he had got our wind. He turned as though he had struck an invisible electric wire. "With no more play left in him, bounding over the dusty plain he went. The dust hung in the air. Now all that was left was the dust trail smoking behind that fleet little wild figure in the distance. All of the scene had been observed from our passing canoe, going on the stream at upwards of ten miles an hour. Although we subsequently saw other caribou on the Colville River trip, none of the others gave us the show that this one did.

We would not kill fresh meat at this time. Our stomachs were full, and our canoe was very full; we had a lot to handle

In watching our navigation every minute on the strange river and we had little intention of killing anything at all while we were traveling rapidly down it. Numbers of lost opportunities of different sorts soon fell behind our track as the ceaseless flood grappled with us; many a time when we got going on it, we just couldn't stop! Shooting from a moving boat is not the best way to select and kill a fat caribou in strange country. The old bulls would of course have a good layer of back fat at this season. They would soon be at their very best of all the year. Our mouths watered, in a way, whenever we saw one. Yet we did not fire our rifles at all along this river, and as for the geese well, they were too cute to eat! It was good not to hunt now. Hunting would begin all too soon in order to live. All humane explorers and travelers should depend in summer entirely on their fish nets. Would our nets prove to us that there were fish to eat in this unknown arctic river? What kind of fish?

We had been noticing streaks along the face of the cliffs. They were black, set in yellow, when the sun hit them, and ranged from a few inches in thickness up to six feet, I judged. "Connie, that looks like coal to me," I finally told her.

We could see these veins of coal only from a distance for some time. It was difficult and dangerous to come too near the cliffs, for their perpendicular nature combined with the rock slides and the fast water eating at them to make it likely that a canoeist might have a few tons of earth dumped into his lap at any time. Eventually we made a successful landing and looked about. Yes, the seams whose wavy lines beautified the cliff face certainly were coal, beyond a doubt. Piles of coal had slithered down the chutes from the veins above and could be picked up at the base of the cliffs wherever they were not dumped straight into the river, as many hundreds of tons doubtless are each summer.

Connie wanted to get right out and grab some coal, but I told her to hold the canoe. Then I stepped out in my hip boots and immediately sank to the knees in ooze. Mosquitoes swarmed out then from the sheer face of the cliff itself, and I stood there holding lumps of coal in my hands.

We didn't take any coal in the canoe because it would have got the canoe dirty, and mostly because we had no room for it. We never cooked with it, although we know of those who have; this coal is well known to arctic coast inhabitants. Its existence is also mentioned in certain technical bulletins of the United States Geological Survey and the Bureau of Mines as seen by less than a half dozen men who have been here. Yet the extent of the coal, petroleum, and all other minerals remains completely unknown in our arctic lands as yet, and it can only be guessed as to how far they may possibly be developed in the years to come.

The coal seams continued with us about a hundred miles. In an exposed two-hundred-foot perpendicular cliff, for example, would be the following layers: ten feet down from the prairie surface might be a seam a foot wide; six inches lower, then, a seam four inches wide; eight feet below that might come six seams, ranging from two inches to two feet wide, spaced like chocolate icing on a many-layered white cake; next there might be a break of twenty feet, and the whole would be repeated again. Last of all would come the big seam from six to eight feet thick in the best places. This would naturally lead the observer to think that there possibly lay thicker seams deeper down into the earth. It was soft coal, not so many years old, as geological age is counted.

It was near midnight when we saw a rather large river, tinkling over furrowed gravel, by three different mouths, into the Colville. Beneath the circling sun a mother and father Canada goose guarding a whole family of little goslings honked loudly and retreated up a backwater among dazzling green foliage as I drove tent stakes. Bumblebees bumbled over the flowers standing motionless on their stalks beside our small tent, the mosquitoes roared, and it was so stifling hot that we longed within our head nets for a breath of cool air. This, we guessed correctly, was the junction of the Anaktuvuk River. In Eskimo it means Defalcation Place.

The procedure of tying our canoe was a little different here from anything we had ever done before. There was absolutely nothing to tie the canoe to no trees, not even a sizable rock. Yet we must tie it somehow. Should our canoe ever get away with our equipment in it as we slept, well we would not be in a position to extricate ourselves and neither would there be another human being on earth aware of our predicament. To lose one's canoe or equipment is inexcusable. This was a vacation much like anyone might take anywhere as far as the problems of camping went, except that here tragedy could easily stalk the heels of a camper who allowed himself little carelessness. In these things a human being is, of course, his own worst enemy. We must neither break, abuse, nor lose any smallest item of our carefully packed equipment in that fourteen-foot canoe while traveling the arctic coast of America.

To secure the canoe I tied its lead rope to the center of a canoe paddle and laid the paddle up on shore, at right angles to the rope, where I buried it carefully under small rocks. I did this again with the stern rope and the second paddle. It is surprising how solid a tie-up one can make with a few rocks in this manner. If only sand were present, as was the case after we emerged from the Anaktuvuk Plateau onto the

Coastal Plain, where I dug a trench a foot deep and buried the paddles which held the canoe's tie ropes. In this manner the whole thing looked like two capital T's. With a tie like this at either end of a canoe which is already hauled up on shore as far as you can get it, you can sleep a deal more soundly than you would otherwise. An extremely solid anchor can be made in this way in the softest sand. It is impossible to pull such an anchor loose from the proper angle: the rope will break first.

It can be seen that when we camped, we did not want to unload everything we had from the canoe, for this included gasoline and ammunition for a year, besides certain equipment for winter like snowshoes and a meat grinder handy arctic items, both of them. The contents of the canoe were protected from rain by canvas.

Of course, the airplane had set us down on the Colville with many a nice item missing from our outfit. Among these were the ridgepole and uprights for pitching the tent. Formerly, we could always cut new poles at any time in the forest when we camped. Now, in reducing our flying weight to get over the divide, we could not afford to bring tent poles. I trusted that the Colville might supply new tent poles, and it did! They were limber and sagged in the middle, but we were thankful to secure them at the first camp. We would carry them from here on down to the Arctic Ocean with us.

Meantime Connie packed all the camp gear we would use up to the spot where I set up the tent. The flowers there made our front yard look like a garden. "It's all right that the ridge pole sags at that," I said, "because I see right now, we're going to have to pitch our tent low so as to pile rocks or sods on the bottom flaps to keep the mosquitoes out. Hand me the shovel and I'll cut some sods now."

Mosquitoes were crawling under our head nets and onto our wrists between glove and cuff; we worked fast ashore while the sweat poured down. The creatures of the arctic regard the mosquitoes of summer as a far greater menace than they do the short winter days The family of geese in the little eddy of the Anaktuvuk River were not bothered by the insects at all; their plumage made them immune. How we envied them their tranquility in this paradise! The caribou probably envied them too, for the herbivores suffer seriously from mosquitoes and flies, the insect plague being one reason why the caribou hung along the banks of the river and were often on the run.

It is always an interesting fact that while we are in mid-stream

Connie and I talk about the elaborate meal we will have when camp is made, but when that time comes and we crawl inside the sealed tent with our water bucket, the grub box and mosquito spray gun, and raise our head nets at last, the meal is simple to say the least; in fact one is lucky to get anything to eat all. Tonight, for instance, what would it be? The very thought of enduring the heat of the camp stove inside the tent made cooking untenable so long as anything remained to eat cold. We could get fuel if we wanted it little masses of willow roots could be seen caught upon the Anaktuvuk's furrowed gravel, and we had carried other small sticks along with us in the bow of the canoe all day as we traveled; yet neither did we feel inclined to set up the stove outside the tent among the mosquito hordes. Every item we cooked would be full of bugs. We only wanted to get inside the tent and be left alone from that continuous tap tapping on our jackets, the all-pervading roar in our ears of those billions of wings. No, we wouldn't cook at all on such a night. We would live on cold snacks, on all our luxuries eaten straight down, until we could collect our resources! Why, that's just the way the natives do!

As the spray gun did its work inside the tent and its pungent droplets sifted gently down into the grub box and water bucket and we lifted our nets to take our first good look at each other in a number of days, Connie set out a jar of jam and the dirty bag containing our old last winter's dried caribou meat. And as usual, something was forgotten that should have been brought from the canoe.

"Oh, the bread, dear. I forgot all about the bread. Would you mind going out to get it from the canoe?"

"Let it stay. I wouldn't brave those bugs again for a ten course dinner." Yes, it is true that once you get safely ensconced inside the tent you think twice about leaving it again in mosquito land.

We ate dried meat, therefore, with straight jam for dessert. This is a rather typical meal of arctic river travelers in the summertime, it seems to me, and so I mention it.

I laid out the sleeping bag, erected the bed net; then I peeked out the tent flap one last time before turning in. Already, new mosquitoes were filtering in as the fumes from incense died on its little trays beside us. The first day on the Colville River was ended. The family of geese swam beside our canoe, eying it; the white jaw straps of the parent geese gleamed in the midnight sun. Beyond were those distant bluffs, stepping onward, on to the polar sea. We were content. As we slept, the *Little Willow* rode serenely, tied bow and stern, mirrored in the peaceful arctic river, while the sun rolled along the flawless horizon like a golden ball.

Mathew's people dressed in winter clothes for us

Mathew and his grandchild

2

The blue river wound over the stony horizon. The cliffs and scalloped buttes, the romantic headlands, were fading. They no more flashed by like a rock-studded belt; they were going, going, gone. The river sprawled out onto the Arctic Coastal Plain, a mile wide, deep, full, and serene. We kept traveling steadily, realizing that if the winds arose, they could hold us up for days. The rapids were over now and only memories. Navigation from here on to the ocean should be a simple matter so far as the dangers of violent currents were concerned, for the pace slackened out at once. We began to wonder how far away the ocean was. Probably not more than thirty miles by air distance.

There are very perceptible differences in climate and vegetation even so far inland as fifteen miles from the coast of the Arctic Ocean. How could we know it? This was our last really tropical day for the next year.

So far, we had seen no sign of human beings other than an old abandoned shack. "Do you think it is possible we might find Eskimos living below, right on this very river, that nobody knows anything about?" we began to ask each other. We had decided that it just was possible we might find Eskimos along the coast of the ocean near the river's mouth. We had to find them eventually, of course, although upon a day like this in hot summer the future was something one couldn't waste time worrying about. There was too much to enjoy here and now.

The underwater exhaust of our little motor was so silent that we could talk with ease while we traveled. A great expanse of gravel bar, miles long, stretched down the featureless horizon on both sides of us while the water level surged even with the level of the land. The willows had shrunk down to only two feet in height, and finally nothing at all grew taller than six inches. As for fuel to burn, there is a great deal more of that on this prairie than the newcomer realizes at a glance. Fuel can be secured for the little sheet iron stove in the form of roots sticking out of mounds or banks when one knows how to look for them, and you learn to cook a whole meal with just a few twigs, or even with Cassiope, a heather which can be burned. We should have to get over some of our inland notions derived from areas where there is much fuel, and get used to new ways.

The Colville River sprawled aimless and gigantic through the Arctic Coastal Plain in the serene sunshine, when right on top of the endless gravel bar which stretched ahead of us a far black dot caught our eye. I took up the binoculars at once. "It looks like one of those fifty-five-gallon gas drums drifted down the river and lodged there, is all I can figure," I told Connie. "It must have floated down from Umiat on the spring flood." We thought of the possibility of there being some few quarts of gasoline still left in it. Now there would be a nice find! Whatever it was, the object looked artificial on the landscape.

We rode on for half an hour and that gasoline drum on the distant plain still looked just about the same size. Funny country, different from what you were used to—you just couldn't tell if you were looking at a small object close up or a large object far in the distance. I knew right then that that object was no gasoline drum. It must be bigger than we had at first thought, and seen from far away. And it must be man-made. "Look again, Bud," and once more I brought the glasses to bear upon it. This time there could be no mistake. It was a house! Square, too, and seemingly covered with tar paper!

"A house!" echoed Connie. "I don't know a lot about Eskimos yet, but that looks like the work of a white man to me. Let me see!"

"The people are at home this time, too," I was able to tell fifteen minutes later, as Connie sat beside me speculatively. "There is a little white tent a couple of miles below it."

It was just possible those people we saw had some sort of binoculars or glasses handed down from the old seafarers who once plied this

The Colville River

coast, and were watching us too, I thought—if I could guess anything about either an arctic or a seafaring people. This proved to be entirely correct. Almost all arctic dwellers, either Eskimo or white, have some kind of glasses which are second only to their rifles in making their living on the prairie and on the sea.

The house which had looked like a gas drum became a twelve-by-sixteen-foot tar-papered shack in due time. We had long minutes to discuss it; its shape reminded one of the old-fashioned chicken coop, but sincerely believed that Connie's first flash impression was essentially correct that no Eskimo would erect a dwelling so high and square against the winds, and that it had been built by a white man. It had. It was a little trading post for several years before our arrival in the arctic, and the lone white man, Jack Smith, who built it he and his kind being now long forgotten lost $30,000 here in this particular arctic investment in the trading for white foxes with the Eskimos. No one was living in this establishment, which loomed gaunt and vacant on the plain as we passed it by. But the two little white tents below gave evidence of the presence of actual living people here of the kind that prefer a tent to a house: our first real arctic Eskimos!

People poured out of the little tents. We thought they would never stop coming out. Finally. about fifteen people were in sight, standing on the riverbank in a solid block. Through the glasses we could see figures break away from the block and run back and forth. We had been sprucing up and this was just what the Eskimos were doing before we arrived!

The little group may not have seen anybody at all in some months, and they seemed quite as happy to see new people as we were.

A whaleboat drawn up on the beach gave a decidedly oceanic flavor to the inland pastoral scene; its tall mast equipped for a sail and its graceful curving hull spoke of the sea. The Arctic Ocean could not be more than fifty river miles away; this turned out to be an accurate guess, at that. As we drew near. we saw broad, tanned, smiling Eskimo faces in splashes of color from what were to us exotic costumes. These faces had a broad jawline and character to them·when one crosses the Arctic Divide. he makes a complete transition, not only in geography but in the culture of the people. The transition, because of the special fuel and clothing problems involved north of the timber line, has not been made by many in this way: you belong either to the one side or to the other, and you don't know how to live in the other land across the mountain chain.

We concentrated on making our landing, and as we did so the women and young girls of the group broke forward from the little rise on which the tents were situated and led the way to meet us. This was entirely different from what the forest Indian women would do.

"Now you must talk to the women and leave me to the men," I had lectured Connie. She had never paid enough attention to the native women, it seemed to me, because, as Connie said, so often the women were shy, or they spoke no English and would not talk at all. It was from the men that we always got all of our information on travel conditions which an explorer wants to know, and Connie liked to speak up to the men and ask questions, rather to my discomfort at times. She liked being an explorer.

But here things were different. These Eskimo girls and women were real huskies and they had a frank way about them which was neither silly nor shy. By temperament Eskimo people are more fun-loving and friendly than natives we had so far known, and the women, as Connie said, were more "emancipated." First, we stood on the beach and shook hands with the total membership of the straightforward family, from the oldest man down to the youngest child in arms. But what then of our questions which we wanted to ask them about life on the Colville River, and about the location of the Arctic Ocean? We had no sooner shaken hands all around than we saw that these people spoke no English. And we didn't know a word of Eskimo.

Out of the corner of my eye I saw the feminine athletes of the tribe and numbers of scrambling excited children conducting Connie up the embankment in royal escort. This was to meet their mother. The old matriarch of what was a large compound primitive family, all of whom were related to each other in some way, sat cross-legged on a caribou skin outside the entrance to the tent, complacently chewing on a long-stemmed pipe carved from a willow. Her ancient face was a mass of wrinkles as she beamed forward, wreathed in smiles. She offered her hand and chattered very rapidly in what seemed to be sharp, witty overtures, but did not rise. Then, breaking out in a cough which exploded unpleasantly into the visitor's face, she pawed into her voluminous skirts and brought forth a beaded hide tobacco pouch and filled up for a smoke. Connie observed that the shreds of tobacco left in the pouch were mighty few; she was glad she wouldn't have to smoke a pipe of peace as the heartier adventurers of other days did in our West. A more practical thought for today's traveler was that although we had brought some tobacco with us into this country, we, alas, felt that we had none to spare at the present time to help out the old crone, inasmuch as we thought it wise to conserve it for dealing with later Eskimos.

Such was our introduction to Matthew's People. They have their Eskimo names. but they have their English names too, by which we find it most simple, for the convenience of this story, to call most of our Eskimos today. They are listed in the United States Bureau of the Census and are American citizens. They range through the hinterlands several hundred miles distant from Point Barrow, whose draft district during the war encompassed 60,000 square miles. Some of their sons served in the late war. But most moderns I suppose are not intimately acquainted with Matthew's People and ones like them, and so we hope to present them as they really are. Old Matthew and his people are mighty likable people to me, and I felt quite at home with them, while I think I understand something of their ways.

How beautiful were their furs! They were all dressed in fur parkas! To us this was remarkable beyond belief. Sweat cascaded in rivers down their amiable faces in the heat! Why the furs in summertime, on a day like this? One reply could be that north coast Eskimos wear fur next to the skin almost all the year around, and that we had simply entered a new country where we were brought up against different customs of dress. In this country the wise person is never far from his furs at any time, even in the summer—remember that! In this costume was to be found the influence of the real arctic climate which we had never seen before.

A second explanation is that the parkas are a protection against the mosquitoes. For this family possessed but scant white man's apparel or cloth known as "calico." Having little or no calico, the primitive Eskimo in summer has no other recourse than to wear his oldest skins which are worn thin so that he may be cool.

But these weren't old clothes! I know that now. These were best clothes, winter clothes, and terrifically hot! The reason for all these tall wild wolf and wolverine hoods, drawn up over polite but agonized faces which poured out the oil, was—should we say it?—a very human kind of vanity They put on their best winter clothes when they saw us coming up on the horizon miles away, so that we would have a good opinion of them.

Later we were to confirm a hundred times over what we might now suspect—that Eskimos are a very vain people about their clothing and personal appearance, as they see it. No more sophisticated people in all the world are more particular about these things. Number one observation: if we have the idea that Eskimos or any primitive dwellers have no pride about the things we take pride in, we are all wrong. Social events in their lives, no matter how insignificant they may seem to us, are just as important to them, according to their lights, as they are to the wealthiest social matron in the midst of the most fashionable whirl, and Eskimos worry just as much as we do about what the neighbors think of them!

Matthew's People had dressed up for this occasion. With caribou robes worn fur side next their chests, they had drawn on their brightest calico print snow shirts or aitichiluks to cover the tanned caribou hides which made up their wardrobe. In the case of the women, these calico dresses fitted over the outside of longer fur dresses trimmed with wolverine which came down below the knees. Different designs in colored ruffles were sewed to their outer calico dresses, no two alike. In the case of the men, the garments were much shorter, similar to our sport jackets, and they wore plain skin trousers or denim work pants beneath. The calico print aitichiluks of both men and women, which are worn outside their furs, have a dual purpose in modem arctic life: they break the wind and they protect the fur garment from driving snow in the wintertime hence the term "snow shirt." Again, they protect the fur garment from dirt, for they can be laundered with soap and water. People who possess a plentiful supply of calico have several changes of these domestically made snow shirts in different colors, all cut to the scale of their parkas and equipped, of course, with calico hood to cover the hood of the parka as well, except for the fur trim which sticks out around the face and shows on hem and cuffs. This is about the simplest way I can think of to describe it. It is a very becoming costume to them, which these people wear with great grace and a natural sense of art and design. The shame is that they never look so well again if they take up wearing our clothing—which seems to be true of native people almost everywhere.

No colorful calico was wasted on either the old people, who were content to wear the plainest of skins, or the numerous children. The young people of courting age wore the fancy duds. One set of dirty unwashed hides each was all the clothing the children possessed in the world, without a rag of cloth to their names Diaper problems were nonexistent in the case of smaller tots, because they all had the seats of their skin trousers cut out in the shape of a heart. Native Eskimo children run about with no seat to their pants until about the age of six. In winter presumably, they keep warm enough while inside the house and when they go out to play, they have a longer outer parka which hangs down like a flap over the exposed area.

The footwear of the Eskimos is perhaps the most interesting of all. We had read of it in arctic journals, but had little idea of what it was like. The feet of all the young adults were clad in fancy mukluks, as white men have erroneously learned to call any fur boot in Alaska that natives make. The native people possess and use many different types of boots, dependent on the season and the locality, and in their own language they have a different name for each, but mukluk will do for us. The soles of some of the adults' mukluks were not even soiled because they were so new, but the children's and old people's plain hide boots were all but worn out and quite unadorned.

Never again for a whole year on the Eskimo coast would Connie or I see a pair of shoes. Not only are the people unacquainted here with what white men's boots are, but such boots are of no more use as soon as we could, for nothing is more clumsy, cold, and miserable than these when you compare them to the warm, feather-light wading boots of the Eskimo, made of seal! There is no climate anyplace on earth that makes such demands for various footwear as the arctic, but the Eskimos have solved the problem for each condition and season. The civilized footwear of the commercial tanner, like commercially tanned skins, is utterly useless here. Commercially tanned hide, because of the oil in it, is solid in the lower temperatures and cannot be used. Shoes are the one item the arctic coastal dweller can do permanently with out and will never need. The Eskimos' own soft footwear and soft caribou skin clothing have been called the most ingenious in the world. It is a real tragedy that they have almost disappeared today. Wherever the Eskimos have settled in villages, taking on the helplessness of the white in their environment.

What were these people living on here? In their camp they had not a drop of any civilized food which we could see, not even coffee or tea or salt. They were ichthyophagi or fish eaters. Their fish racks were heavy with great oily whitefish, drying in the sun. They were caribou hunters who otherwise live exclusively off the herds of the prairie, and there is no technical word for this that I know of, although perhaps there should be.

Caribou compose three quarters of the Eskimo diet in north Alaska throughout the year, and we can now say that it takes about one hundred caribou during the summer alone to keep a crowd of this size and their dog teams going; out of the kill they are enabled to make their essential winter clothing. Securing skins for clothing was mainly what these people were doing now. Three or four young hunters with rifles did all of the killing for the family. For there is one unfortunate qualification about life as lived in caribou skins: the hair sheds with use until soon the hide is almost bare, and each person must have a complete new set of caribou skin clothing made once each year. Skins of the right hair length for clothing can be secured in the wild state only during the summertime, during July, August, and perhaps early September, the skins of cows and fawns being most highly prized in the clothing line, although old bulls are prized simultaneously for back fat. The lean cows and fawns killed for skins usually go to the dogs.

In order to get enough skins to clothe the family, more meat than can be eaten accrues, and this is often buried in the ground at the kill, to be packed out later by pack dogs or sledded out after snowfall, or, what is quite as likely, the extra meat in flush times, especially if it is not fat, may simply be left to rot on the prairie. The people prefer a diet of straight good whitefish to lean caribou if it comes to a choice between fat and lean.

At the camp were several complete teams of dogs, eight or nine to the team, around forty dogs in all. There were four grown sons in this group and each had to have his own team for winter trapping activities. There are several ways to work dogs in summer but whether they work or not, they must continue to eat all year. While Indians far from the haunts of the white man seemed to treat their dogs somewhat better—perhaps in view of their utility, or because of the brevity of the summer season here. Modern-day Eskimos own many more dogs than they could afford to feed before they had rifles, and this situation has been likened to a vicious cycle: dogs enable the modern primitive to sled long distances over wider ranges to get more caribou to feed more dogs. Fashion and style play a large part in the dog situation here again, for the family that can afford to own the biggest and fastest dog team commands the greatest social prestige in the eyes of its contemporaries. The dogs of Matthew's People in the summertime we saw tied by trap chains, with the trap jaws biting into the willow roots sticking out of the bank—each dog to his own trap.

One of the first things our eyes lit on was a seal lying on the ground in front of the tent, which had come, we knew, from the sea. Connie and I had never seen a seal before, actually. Only later did we learn that this was a special kind of spotted seal which had been secured from a small colony of them which go inland from the ocean as far up the Colville, in fact, as the Anaktuvuk junction. We noted with the seal some curved women's fish knives with carved ivory handles, covered with bloodstains; they were thrown carelessly on the ground.

There must be thousands of these curved women's knives or uluruks still in active use all over Alaska today. We greatly coveted one, especially one having such a handle of carved walrus ivory, but in five years in Alaska we were never able to secure one by asking the natives, because, native-like, at the times we asked at camps, they never had an extra one to spare.

The hearty group of Eskimos seated Connie and me next to the mosquito smudge burning before the tent and clustered about us, sweating and beaming, and fanning themselves with a driftwood fan. Never in my life, it seemed to me, had I seen any human beings who appeared to be in such great health, judging by their high color and ruddy cheeks. They fingered our hats which we passed around to them, and marveled at our mosquito head nets and rubber hip boots. All over Alaska we have almost never seen a native with a head net on, and these people did not seem to know what one was; mosquitoes bite the native people just as they bite us, but there is reason to believe that constant generations of living with mosquitoes have developed for them somewhat of an immunity to the poison in their bites.

The group seemed delighted and surprised to receive someone coming from the upriver direction. Doubtless all the people they knew came from the sea. How many years they had been hunting and fishing at this spot seasonally before seeing human beings come out of the

Colville from the south, we had no way of knowing then. What we couldn't know was that this group were inland people themselves, having been born on upper headwaters of the Colville, and that it was some of them who had lived in that first old shack we saw. Only in this generation had this family moved toward the sea. Eskimos may be more traveled geographically than is the average person in the United States when it comes to distance, and they know more than you would at first suspect: tales from others have described trees and steamboats and the gardens of white men, but these things mean no more to them than the rice paddies of Asia mean to most of us.

The little boxes supplied Connie and me for seats were of a kind we had seen before. Their lids opened on small hinges and inside were kept the trinkets of the women, each box to its owner, with beadwork, needles, thread, combs, mirrors, bright ribbons, and bobby pins. In this case there was in the box also a Presbyterian hymnal. Point Barrow, with which these people had their only civilized contact for purposes of trade, has been occupied by Presbyterian missionaries for a great many years.

Connie was looking at their trinkets with the young women, trying to get some hint of their contacts with white people. "Point Barrow?" she asked, but received no reaction but blankness and puzzlement. The Eskimos called it by some other name. The old lady had commenced to draw Connie a map in the sand with a stick. One of the younger women hurriedly slammed open her box then and appeared with a bright red pencil which had never been used and a piece of paper which had been saved and treasured from some trader's discarded account book. The grandmother, chattering and cackling like a magpie, started in earnest to draw us a map, to the delight and amusement of all who looked on. Connie was really getting somewhere!

On this map was carefully penciled the word WE as our present location, then the course which we should take on the river below us to Beechey Point, which we knew lay along the arctic coast towards Canada. One by one the younger men and women took turns with the pencil to inscribe something on the old lady's map which he or she remembered, to make it clear for us. We knew from our general information that Beechey Point, named after that Captain Beechey who discovered Point Barrow over a hundred years ago, lay along our way, after we reached the ocean, and now we knew from the actions of the Eskimos that they considered this to be a very important place; the sun rose and set around it for them. We heard the term "Beechey Point" over and over in their conversation. This would mean that undoubtedly more Eskimos were living there. This was what we wanted to know!

A young woman took the pencil and drew a picture of a tiny house in between us and our destination, and said clearly, "People," and Connie and I wrote "People" in there. "People" was signified by the Eskimo name of a place called Oliktok. Oliktok is another landmark along the coast on your way to Beechey Point, but of course it hadn't been on our white man's map at all. This was added to the Eskimo drawn map in round careful penmanship. The junction of the Itkillik River with the Colville below was also indicated to come soon, and the contours of every one of the outlying prairie lakes were shown to us, delightedly sketched in by other members of the excited family; but with these lakes we had no concern.

One little detail they overlooked on this map they drew for our use: they completely left out the Arctic Ocean. To show the way their minds worked, they made no differentiation between where the river ended, and the ocean began so that a stranger might know. The omission of the Arctic Ocean, a rather conspicuous feature to us, probably showed that they took it for granted. It was all of the world where they lived, and they evidently did not imagine the doubts which might trouble a newcomer's mind.

At Oliktok we would find People probably in the east of the delta; "Sara's," they said, and smiled broadly. "Sara's," we repeated, and they beamed. There was no map existent of the Colville delta; our own general map was next to worth less. We knew right now that that delta was going to be a big place—but if somebody named Sara lived right around the corner, and probably even herself traveled up and down this river commonly, it was practically a settled land and we had nothing to worry about. Well, not much, anyway.

Now we could get out our camera maybe and take some pictures. First, even if no words can be understood, a smile goes a long way in speaking the universal language of friendliness, and you can't go too far in meeting the other fellow in his own country. Secondly, we do not get the camera out until a certain point of friendship seems to have been reached. This may take an hour, a day, or a week, but one must learn to take plenty of time with people, for it is very rude to flash a camera in anybody's face without so much as "by your leave," and furthermore, really good studies cannot usually be obtained without the subject's co-operation. To put everybody in a gay mood I first took Connie's picture and she took mine and we shot some film just for fireworks. By that time the people were wild to have their pictures taken, too. The next step is usually a group picture, perhaps with Connie and me both in it too, with the camera operated from a tripod by automatic release. Only after this may come the individual portraits of the old fat woman or the little babies with their slanted eyes, for which we have been longing, fearing every moment that the sun may go under a cloud or the picture get away. All good photography must be done casually and in a spirit of good fun. Best portraits are obtained by requesting that the subject not look directly at the camera but continue whatever work he may be doing, as the purpose of our photography is to tell the story of the people's lives.

Matthew's People were so happy to have their pictures taken that the moment they saw the camera they grabbed their youngsters violently with jerks and cuffs, muttering to them in Eskimo not to cry, which the children didn't, although their lips trembled, and fairly sprang into a block formation with their chests thrown out and their backs straight as ramrods. It took some maneuvering to get them to relax, but is this not precisely how most of us pose when we are going to have our pictures taken?

We walked to our canoe with the entire group. The men were interested in our canoe and equipment but were far too polite to stare at or examine it. But you can bet very few details about us and our outfit escaped their attention. We would not dare encourage or allow the people to touch anything because we were so far from where we could get any repairs if anything went wrong. We believed our little one and-a-half-horse outboard motor would be very likely the only one in the Arctic Ocean, on our side of the world anyway. This guess was not wrong. The Eskimos themselves relied entirely on dog power, man power, and sailing to move about. By summer they have always sailed on this ocean, along its edge, with a square sail of their own invention.

Our friends, Matthew's People, stood on the bank and waved as we pushed off. "It is surprising how well you can carry on a conversation with only smiles, isn't it?" remarked Connie as the little tents began to fade away.

Behind us, diminutive figures, dwarfed by the immensity of the green summer landscape which surrounded them, piled pell-mell into the tent to take off those best, unendurable winter parkas and get cooled off!

The Colville shoaled as we neared the delta

Pack ice closed in with a shift in the wind

3

The Colville River lay before us, broad, still, and asleep. A white-fronted goose rode on the glassy surface with her one gosling kept from sight just in back of her. The gosling couldn't make much speed as I gunned the motor, yet the mother stayed between us and it. At last when we were very near, the gosling dove and, trumpeting, the mother took off. As she cleared the water it was impossible to tell whether the reflected image looked more real, or the actual goose in the air. "I got it, Bud. Boy, what a picture!" The mother goose swung back to her gosling with the low sun painting her with orange light.

At midnight we sighted a group of grave crosses upon a low rolling hill to the east. The hill made you think of green country club golf links, close-cropped. The gravel bars were gone; not a rock of any sort could have been found in miles on the plain. And for some reason, I thought of the low greenness of Holland and its canals. In a while, we were tied up at the mouth of the Itkillik River. With the tent pitched upon shovel and oars, we turned in, while once more the winged summer chorus of the arctic sang us to sleep.

The wind billowed out our tent when we awoke late in bright daylight some twelve hours later. There were big whitecaps running along the point where the two broad canals met, but in our harbor just up the mouth of the Itkillik the *Little Willow* rode securely at anchor. The net we had set wriggled with fish, and we hurried to pull it in preparatory to having breakfast.

"Looks like we'll be here a while. It's no use fighting a head wind. Better save our gasoline. We'll walk over some of these golf links around here in the beginning of the delta today."

Unknown to us, we had made our camp last night right on top of a prehistoric Eskimo town. There were over a hundred grass-grown mounds laid out in regular streets all about us in various stages of decay. Nearest the river were signs of the most recent camps, where, just as we did now, people had lived in their tents.

Like pups taken for a stroll, we burrowed under rubbish and poked about every likely looking ruin. "Here is an old skin boat." Oh, but it wasn't an ancient one at all but a modern one which may have been used by somebody's uncle just last year; we would run across him soon. Its frame was willows tied together with thongs. Its skin was cleverly stitched from common hair seals.

The air was full of bird songs. A black-bellied plover flew up alarmed and kept landing a few yards away, only to fly up with the same forlorn cries all over again. The horned larks sang on the wing, on the downward descent of their flight, as they sprang from the greensward that our feet trod. Wilson snipes gave their high tremulous mellow whistle, filling the vault of the prairie sky from we knew not where. All about us was life of the present, while we walked amid the village of the past.

Connie suggested a flower collection, and we began, systematically for the first time, to see how many varieties we could find. There were big furry flowers that had a blossom as large as a rose, pea-green and velvety; they grew on thick furry stalks as stocky as mushrooms. There were clumps of moss the size of a chair cushion sprinkled with lavender stars—this was no moss at all but a true member of the plant kingdom, reproducing by seeds and not spores.

When our amateurs' collection the day was complete, we had yellow Iceland poppies; a dozen varieties of blue flowers; Indian paintbrushes of three shades; five-petaled anemones. The anemones typify the windflowers which are so frequent on the prairie. These flowers are pollinated by wind; the fact that the majority of arctic flowers have little scent is a hint that they are not dependent upon luring insects for their pollination. Our collection numbered about thirty-five species that day. Quite a few were doubtless unclassified by science, but one we were certain of was our old friend the common dandelion, growing happily and at home, even here.

The Itkillik-pas—mouth of the ltkillik or Indian River, as it means to the Eskimo—seemed to speak of a civilization of the past, and in the wind across the grass was the whisper of a greater civilization to come. But at present the wind and the wild creatures and the two plains' rivers and ourselves were all that were there. Our eight-by-ten-foot tent and our fourteen-foot canoe were mere specks in a land where distances are measured in the thousands of miles and the in habitants can be counted on your fingers.

With the ltkillik-pas begins the delta of the Colville. Our map showed a straight channel below us cutting east down the delta into the ocean. This was the channel we wanted.

"You know I don't believe I've ever seen a river delta before," Connie mentioned as we started down it two days later.

"You'll know more about it soon," was all I could say. I had never seen one to explore either. But I knew we would have to succeed in getting through it; we certainly couldn't get back where we came from. I thought we had better be careful not to go clear out into the ocean in the delta, too. One might easily do this, when you came to think about it. The mouth of a large river in entering the ocean builds up many big islands and mud flats from the silt it drops when the current slackens, and it may build them up far out to sea. We can say now that the delta of the Colville is about twenty miles broad at its front and that the river enters the Arctic Ocean by six different mouths.

"We've got to take every little channel that we find which seems to bear to the extreme east," I warned. Since we were going to go east along the ocean front, going down the east channel of the delta would save us miles. But we hoped there wouldn't be complications. It had to be the far eastern channel and we mustn't miss it. For what might happen to people in their canoe who go too far out into the Arctic Ocean by a large strange river and get lost in some fog or meet some storm rolling in from the sea?

The delta since the last windy day had already become no place for lingering. It was cold! Flowers bloomed as profusely as ever but they had no color beneath the drab sky and there was what would you call it?—a sea breeze. The wind had changed about, the sun was gone. Gone were the friendly perspiring Eskimos we had seen a few miles back in another land, and gone was everything with which we were familiar. A black cloud rolled in, spreading rapidly across all the northern sky, under which we knew lay the ocean.

"What is it?" Connie asked, startled, as the blackness came visibly toward us.

"Fog!"

I can say now that it is indeed quite a transition for an inland people to go down to the arctic coast for the first time. There is really nothing fearful about it, but the conditions are not what you are used to, and it means great changes in your attitudes and outlook to adapt to the world that is there. It's a wonderful world in its own right, and quite pleasant, but you have to have the right clothing, and that we didn't have when we first came down to this sea. We were two timid explorers, wondering what was going to happen next. Our viewpoint is understandable, I suppose, because it was the viewpoint of average people cautiously feeling their way in the unknown.

The little motor continued churning along in deep water by a peat-hung riverbank that led into fog. "Might as well continue on as long as we can," we decided, fixing that peaty riverbank with our eye, so as not to lose it. There is not much use in camping to wait over for better weather when you might wait forever for it; in the delta there was little wood for fuel.

"I think we'll find plenty of wood if we can once get through the delta," Connie surmised. "There should be some driftwood lodged on the beaches along the Arctic Ocean, I think."

"You're making a good guess," I said. "But here in this river delta I suppose we're just about at sea level now, and there isn't any current to bring wood down from above, while the drift of the polar basin naturally can't lodge on the continent where it is guarded by delta islands."

Soon there was so little current left that the river seemed to even be running backwards with the upstream wind. If our motor was cut off, our canoe was blown backwards and no longer drifted forward. Ahead of us loomed such a broad expanse of water that we began to think every hour we were now actually ready to enter the ocean. But this was not so. A turn of our heads was enough to make us see that the ocean for which we were on the lookout lay, to all appearances, right behind us, the vast watery realm from which we had just come. Everything was getting to be just all water.

It was a perfectly miserable day for riding in an open boat. Inside our rubber hip boots our feet were wet; the boots did not leak, but a dampness accumulated inside them from lack of proper foot ventilation. The stiffness and tightness of our apparel, tending to cut off circulation while we sat cramped in the boat, caused us rapidly to become very cold. Fabric clothing and stiff boots do not conserve body heat. But we battled on for a few hours with the result of at least moving our camp a good many miles farther down the delta.

Mirages of the distant fading shore line of the river stretched out into blank nothingness, and still our Eskimo map hinted to me that we probably could not expect to see the ocean for a day or two yet. I was realizing, too, that it was easy to burn up a summer's supply of gasoline, just wound up amid all these delta channels. Some of the channels were sure to be shallow, and on a day of upstream wind you had no current at all to guide your decisions about which channel to take. The broadest channels might lead nowhere. In the cloying fog these aimless channels would wind and wind in circles and figure S's, all over the compass and back again: a most trying situation, which tended to make one a little irritable with it.

Fearful of missing the east channel, we clung to the east shore, searching every shadow of a bay, taking every wildcat slough that came along on that side. We ended up the day stranded in a chain of deep still tundra lakes miles off the highway, in the midst of droves of hobbling geese and piping curlews mixed up with wildflowers. There was no driftwood to burn. There was only a place at the end of the world where ranks of flowers stood in the fog. There was only a howling and hooting from afar out of the great swamps, which ended in a long-drawn eerie wail—the noises made by the arctic loons.

Our feet and hands white and numb with cold, our faces burned raw from facing the wind, our stomachs caving in, we had to turn around then and start back over all those miles and turns to the secondary branch of the main channel we had been following; arriving at the fork again, we took the other turn of the secondary channel and followed it forward, until it, too, split up into lakes.

"Oh, let's not worry about it anymore today," we finally said. "Let's pitch the tent and eat something cold, and we'll figure the fool thing out in the morning." We ate a few dried apricots down like candy, and rolled up in the sack to recuperate.

In the morning I spied a bull caribou on the sky line a half mile away, but Connie, holding the boat's nose, was stuck in the mud and couldn't reach me my gun. By the time a hunt was under way, the fine bull was gone. We were beginning to think about fresh meat absently, or at least the sight of an especially good bull seemed to set off those responses. Living on knickknacks and all the luxuries was likely to lay us on our backs—an indigestible and scurvy diet, which could not be continued forever. We had pretty well learned that store food, without fresh meat to go with it (on a nonvegetable diet), just doesn't go after a few days, luxurious as we had thought such a living might be.

It's a peculiar sensation to be canoeing down a large river with the shore a mile away on either hand and strike bottom. Hungry and suffering from indigestion all at the same time, we couldn't get to shore to even eat! And I think we both had in mind, as we went on, that some of the worst shipwrecks have occurred to much larger vessels than ours when they were caught by a storm in the mouth of a large river just where it empties into the sea.

"I'll bet the waves could get seven feet high here with the water only six inches deep," we commented nervously, as we got out and walked with the boat for a few miles. How we thrashed forward and dragged! How we jumped in the boat again and flailed with our paddles! Being stuck in the shallows will wear a canoeist out worse than anything I know of; of all the problems he will face, lack of water can be one of the most serious. Here our motor was of no use on such abominable mud flats.

Setting our course at last for a group of sand mounds ahead, we reached an island whose, back reared up like a miniature mountain range in the middle of seas of water. From the highest mound, perhaps fifty feet above, I struck an explorer's pose with my binoculars once more.

Miragelike islands floated like low clouds upon the horizon of water. These islands, or perhaps points of the riverbank ahead, were really below our vision around the curve of the earth, but were raised into the sky in distorted shapes and shadows which changed as our position moved. What might have been a white piece of floating ice or a distant sail of a ship out at sea turned out to be a swimming swan near at hand. Caribou tracks plowed a furrow across the eastern bank which had been too shallow for us to reach. There was nothing else. No driftwood, nothing to burn, just nothing. There weren't any mosquitoes any more, for that sea breeze was too cool for them.

As we continued onward, cautiously using the motor from here, in some places the bank of the river disclosed hanging peat ten feet thick, although it was an exception far down the delta when the river's banks were more than four feet above the water surface. High water of storms had cut into the softer soil, washed out the sand, and left the black fibrous peat hanging limply into the river—a common scene along most northern rivers we have seen and along the arctic coast itself, which abounds with "shingle points," as such drooping banks are sometimes called. In such places the story of the past may lie bare and freshly opened by the last flood. Crevasses filled with ice may gleam at you where, sometimes the prehistoric animals are preserved today in their arctic burial grounds. The ancient tropical swamps which once were here lie in the grasp of the last great Ice Age, one foot below the surface, which today in summer is covered smoothly with living soil and flowers and grass. Nature here has the past stored in a great refrigerator. Such rivers as the Colville turn the pages and modern man has but to understand the language and then he will be able to read that great book at will.

Toward the end of our traveling day, a seemingly large slough took off to the east once more and we got into it and followed it. "Wood, Connie! Let's land and warm up!" A nice cache of wood had indeed been bundled into a crack of the bank by the floods these several years past, just in preparation for our coming. It made an extravagant bonfire, considering the circumstances, but our shivering was alleviated, and we were warm for the first time in three days. We walked inland and looked around. Were we on some big island, or what? That you never can go far afoot in such an area as this without finding yourself cut off by icy channels on every side we knew now. We were near the ocean side. No longer was the ground dusty underfoot; it was spongy and moist. Curlews flew up and their long bills flew open and shut as they discussed the unwonted visit of humans here. Pintail ducks and multicolored phalaropes filled every puddle. Little tip ups and other snipes bobbed up and down. A whole raft of mallards and pintails together turned a blue lake into a polka-dotted lake nearby. On all sides of us were limping birds which had suddenly become "cripples" in order to decoy us away from hidden nests.

Ptarmigan rolled away everywhere. I caught a little chick in my hands which was hiding still as death. The little fellow peeped plaintively. Then I saw the parent birds running along the ground—the female, brown and drab, and the male spotted white, with a red mark above his eye. The brightly colored rooster bird cackled and puffed out to twice his size, he stood his ground jauntily as I let his youngster go. The male ptarmigan is an example of nature's great conspiracy. Coincidental with the mating season he becomes a conspicuous feature of the arctic summer landscape, at which time he loses all the brains he ever had in a kind of balmy madness, unconsciously serving the purpose of bait for all lurking enemies.

The pastures of flowers and the winding, bird-crowded channels of the delta in which we were lost for three days comprised a most interesting avian sanctuary. It is one we wish every person might see.

Two swans near our anchored canoe had grown nervous as we returned. With a running start, like seaplanes they left the water. With graceful necks outstretched, they became white arrows tipped with a black point as they swung by us calling. It was a queer call for such a large bird—high-pitched and given in a most timid, inquiring manner.

Yes, the delta of the Colville is a maze of lakes and wet fog, and winding water channels. The channel we were on narrowed, was joined by another that was deep and narrow, and soon the same old thing happened. The color of the water cleared to crystal depths, telling us we couldn't get out to the ocean this way; around the bend was a big still lake once more: dead end.

We pitched the tent and set up the stove, having brought along some sticks in our canoe. A warm tent and hot tea made us feel cheerful about the whole thing. Connie relaxed on her caribou robe which represented the backs of four caribou she had killed far from here and was reminded of a summer she had spent at a girls' camp. "Oh, we're jolly campers!" she sang, full of loyalty to that early time.

"Have a heart," I said.

"Anyway, it's nice to know the country is inhabited and we'll meet Sara pretty soon, I think," Connie yawned complacently while sodden snowflakes plumped against the tent outside and melted into the lonely prairie grass.

4

The problem of finding our way out to the Arctic Ocean and incidentally to Sara's house had us not exactly worried, but impatient, after following so many channels that split so many ways. We were five days in the delta altogether before we found our way out of it.

Next morning the sky was clear, however, and as Connie and I cooked up some rice on our camp stove inside the tent, I walked about with the best of anticipations. Perhaps what we needed was a young goose to eat. We were half sick from living on condensed foods, which will kill a person in a short time, so to speak. I came to a sharp bank pitching down the prairie. Below lay a lake with a stream flowing through it, and as I stepped up some fifty families of geese, both white fronted and Canadians, flopped alarmed into the stream. A group of goslings fell over the embankment near me to join the main flock. They looked so ridiculous! The geese couldn't get over thirty yards away from me because the lake was so small, and because of the ever-present menace of the eagles they did not want to leave it. Perhaps three hundred gabbling geese in all, from those newly hatched on up to big buxom feathery adults, were here. They filled the lake to capacity and filled the air with a terrific din. Goose meat for dinner? Well, maybe tomorrow. I couldn't shoot into those nice ridiculous geese and break up that scene. We ate highly spiced meat out of a can again. We could appreciate the indigestion of the Army and the Boy Scouts on long reconnaissance.

The wiles of the nearby ocean had been at work while we had slept in the tent. Our canoe sat clear out of the water, while only a trickle marked the channel of yesterday: another one of the deceptions of camping in a river delta. The storm tide had gone out and left us dry.

As a matter of fact, the Arctic Ocean has almost no tides. And this is one of the reasons why we had thought we could canoe on it as people cannot expect easily to do on other oceans.

It was largely on the basis of the lack of tides of the Arctic Ocean that several years ago most scientists held to the theory that some great unexplored and unknown land must lie north of Alaska, or that the Beaufort Sea must be landlocked on all sides. This land has proved to be nonexistent and the action of the tides in the Arctic Ocean, or rather their almost complete absence on our side of the world, must be accounted for in other ways. I do not pretend to account for it except to say that this ocean is landlocked by all of the continents generally and to mention that the moon, which influences the tides of all the world, behaves differently in arctic regions. Anyway, there you have it: an ocean that doesn't behave as other oceans do.

The fluctuation of the daily sea level amounts to not more than two feet, the lowest stage occurring at the time of the northeasterly winds and the highest stage on the southwesterly winds. However, there are some "storm tides" on occasion which do not behave on schedule, and after a storm the water may make such a drop as would affect a person's canoe some what.

In a few miles of travel, we were able to join the main river. The day was calm. We must enter the ocean on such a day as this; now was the time. Ahead of us, queer islands and the other distant shore line of the river's mouth floated out into the sky. Some points were fat and squat, while others stretched tall and thin. Through the binoculars they appeared the same as they did to unaided vision, except that the powerful glasses, in penetrating the miles of different layers of air heated to varying degrees, caused the whole queer scene to shimmer and tremble in waves. If a breeze was blowing, all landmarks of any sort, or shadows of landmarks, would lean over in the direction in which the breeze was blowing! This is a typical condition on the low Arctic Coastal Plain in summer. It is even more emphasized when one is on a large body of water in a small boat in these regions.

Following one's nose through such a realm of shadows and mirages, one seemed to be just hanging in space between heaven and earth, and nothing seemed real. What kind of place was this? On this balmy day, now that the wind had dropped, and the soft scents were borne from the continent outward, one had that sense of adventure of being just about to enter a totally different environment, whatever it turned out to be.

The water was shallow; the river lay a mile wide, and just a few inches deep, level all the way across. What had happened, of course, was that in our anxiety we had kept all the time too far to the east, and we had missed the real east channel, by which the Eskimos traveled, altogether. Here it was too shallow to use the kicker and we paddled on, scraping bottom and fighting it out to the last. Eventually the thin line of the miragelike shore on our west side ran out to sea and faded entirely. To our east or right hand lay a low shore two miles away, which was as close as we could get to it, while rolling combers of a new rhythm gently washed the *Little Willow*'s sides; as we shoved with our oars, we could practically see the bottom between waves.

We must get out of here! What if we got washed further aground and couldn't get off with our heavy load? What if a good storm should start blowing in from the sea? Was this the Arctic Ocean yet? We didn't even know!

Slowly the water began to deepen. Slowly it crept up over my canoe paddle when I poked down, and up to the deep enough mark where I knew the kicker would work. An out board motor on a boat at a summer resort is one thing, but the same motor when it is your only source of power on the whole Arctic Ocean is another. I primed it carefully. With a single pull on its starter rope, the good little kicker took off. We could charge each wave with power! Gone was the helpess feeling. We could deal with this Arctic Ocean now.

We believe we entered the Arctic Ocean at just about five o'clock of one late July afternoon, but we can never be sure of the hour. Like many of life's great events it was a gradual sort of thing, a kind of development. "Let's taste the water." But it was sweet. Of course, you would expect the water in the ocean to be sweet rather than salty for quite a few miles around the mouth of a large river. And Sara was living some place right along here! This made the event of our first embarkation upon the polar sea not only normal but matter of fact. We had known it all along: there is hardly any place in the world that you can't find people living.

Such a string of low islands or sand reefs run along our north Alaskan coast that a stranger might well be troubled to say just where the Colville River leaves off and the Arctic Ocean really begins. This is another factor, besides the lack of tides, which stands the canoeist in good stead. A canoeist can canoe in what we learned is called locally the "lagoons" which lie inside the islands. Here he is protected from the actual open sea for much of the way along the coast. As a matter of fact, it is standard policy to use very small boats in this ocean. Since the continental shelf is shallow, big vessels can't move easily, and not at all until late in the summer. A fourteen-foot canoe can travel within the lagoons along the coast in faster time and earlier in the season than the most powerful icebreaker ever invented. So much for the advantages of a canoe in the Arctic Ocean.

The ice within the lagoons thaws weeks and even months before the ice outside the islands can move out; the lagoons are soon comparatively ice free from the warm water pouring off the land. By summer along our north shore, this ocean hardly looks like an ocean at all, but on a calm day is more like a great enclosed millpond.

And a final factor of advantage: the condition of calmness of the Arctic Ocean, while not universal, is strongly accentuated in a peculiar way. There may be only a narrow line of water between the shore and the polar ice pack which lies not far offshore. The very presence of the ice, with its great weight, keeps this ocean calm. Of course, there may be gales, and in the summer the ice pack may go at times as far as a hundred miles offshore from some parts of the continent, but nevertheless the presence of the ice is a very beneficial factor. Along the edge of this ocean you can pitch your camp at all times, just as you would do upon the grassy shores of a lake. It is doubtless a good deal safer than our larger lakes.

Now as we entered the ocean in the calm of evening, we found ourselves cast out upon a vast and magical expanse of water which was colored deep pink by the sky. The low shore line was pink, too, and the twittering of birds was brought to our ears. The next thing we thought after tasting the water was to look around for ice. "Where's the ice that is supposed to be around here?" we asked ourselves jubilantly. "Where are the polar bears?" There wasn't a cake of ice to be seen anywhere and that polar bears could live around here seemed doubtful at this time. Of course, the ice and the bears were out to sea in summer.

For an hour we traveled before the water deepened sufficiently to allow us to approach shore. The shore line had floated like a suspended shadow. When we got to it, it was real, all right, but it was only two to four feet high. It drooped with peat and resembled the bank of a lake or the bank of any northern river. Such did we find the ocean of no tides and no beaches.

We made a landing for a much-needed lunch of warmed over beans and tea. But we could have a fire with ease now; there was plenty of fuel for the needs of camping. Yes, we had guessed right, fortunately: wood does come down the major rivers of the continents, just as you would know if you stopped to think about it, and it floats around the polar basin until it lodges on the shore. Some beaches are better for wood than others, due to the currents; one soon gets to know them. All kinds of wood and all kinds of things in general come down the rivers, but for the present I shall only say that as for fuel, I was relieved when I once got a representative view of the ocean front, and as for housing materials, I felt I could build us a home for winter most anyplace along here, from drift and sods. There were still those caribou tracks, too, coming right up to the edge of the ocean, and as caribou mean food and clothing to the arctic dweller, whatever had one to worry about?

Connie was delighted to learn that the flowers were here, too, that they went right down to the water's edge, not more than a few feet removed from the icy spray. Many flowers were burned in our campfire where we cooked our first pot of tea, using ocean water or Colville River water, for our cooking.

This was the Arctic Ocean all right. I wanted to camp for a sleep at the first likely looking creek mouth we might come to, where we could park the boat, but Connie said thoughtfully, as a bumblebee winged its way over the water across the bow of our moving canoe: "I don't know. Maybe we better push on a bit while this weather holds, and play our luck."

We were tired, after our fight to get through the delta, but something made us hesitate to stop. We wanted to see Sara. There had been something unreal about all this. Maybe she would make us feel more real. Perhaps we had been subconsciously expecting an arctic blizzard or a polar bear to welcome us. Or perhaps we expected something to stop us. However, that might be, flowers bloomed, although snowflakes had fallen only yesterday; the bees buzzed, and the sea was like glass, while birds called continually. I looked through the binoculars and saw only more of the same thing. Except there was a little dog sled left by someone along the miles of empty shore line ahead. It was turned up on its back, runners in the air, like some abandoned child's toy. It spoke of some Eskimo who had dropped that sled just as it was, and it was a real sled! When the snow gave out in this area, not many weeks ago, either.

Five hours after we entered the ocean, at around 10 P.M., a dot appeared upon the long coast in the distance. This must be Sara's house! When we drew nearer two tents were to be seen, also near the house.

I maneuvered the canoe so as not to hit the people's fish net which was set out before their door, and we landed. There were four Eskimos standing on the beach to welcome us. They looked hardly real. They looked like little furry dolls against the still pink summer ocean and the immense backdrop of gravel and sky. Here were the same costumes which had amazed us before. A feature which added to the unrealness of the fur-clad figures was that they had drawn their arms inside their parkas as they stood there, and this left their sleeves dangling limp as puppets' limbs might be, with tall hoods all out of proportion.

Alice, the mother, introduced herself, with the showing of a smile but with eyes narrowed to slits of suspicion. There was Ruth, her grown daughter of twenty, Wilbur, age eleven, and some miscellaneous smaller children in skin tatters. This was Cyrus's camp, we learned. We had understood the name "Cyrus" for Sara's, and Cyrus was a man and the father of this family. He was gone inland hunting caribou when we arrived, which left only the woman and the children at home. "Come in," said Alice, making some show of hospitality. "Please excuse my poor English. I do not speak English very well."

But we were extremely pleased with Alice's English. It certainly sounded good to us! She was part white and she had had twelve years' schooling at the government school at Point Barrow, years ago when she was a young girl. Now she had not been to Barrow for a long time. Alice's facial expression, as we came to know her later that year, was always as it was now. It was an expression of chronic discontent, and her marriage to the man Cyrus had made a union of probably the most improvident Eskimo family on the entire north coast of Alaska. Individual Eskimos, like all people, are different from each other, and this camp was as different from Matthew's happy camp as black is from white.

Alice led the way and we followed her to shelter as gratefully as lost sheep. But it was not to the house we had seen from afar that she led us. Had we expected, after all our experience, to be entertained in the house? Well, yes, naturally; where we come from people usually live in houses and it's rather hard to get over it. Especially by the side of the Arctic Ocean one would imagine a house to be convenient. Of course, we knew the Indians over on the Koyukuk and Yukon usually pitch their tents each summer right outside their own front doors, for they prefer to live in a tent rather than in their perfectly good log cabins during the summer season, but my goodness! doesn't it get a little chilly in the winter over this way if you don't have a house? But these people seemed to look at the matter differently. It was past our comprehension when Alice explained in clear English that the family lived (eight all told) in one of the seven-by-nine-foot tents. That sod and driftwood house over there? Oh, they never lived in that. It turned out to be an icehouse!

It seems the Eskimos are very particular about drinking ice water all the year around, and there are consequently several "ice cellars" at Oliktok belonging to various families, for the storage of meat underground and ice blocks during the hot season. The season is quite hot incidentally, having an average daily temperature on the coast of forty degrees, with occasional variations to fifty degrees and thirty degrees during the more sweltering months of June, July, and August. This frame shack had been erected consequently at some time in the past over one of the principal ice cellars, and Cyrus and Alice were at this time camping alongside and using ice and snow from inside the old wreck of a house (the snow having blown in during the winter and still remaining in the shelter of its walls) for their household and drinking water.

The family did not have an ice cellar of their own, but camped by the several ice cellars here belonging to relatives. Oliktok is a historical fishing site of great excellence, and while other more provident families were living on caribou at this season and getting skins for winter clothing, this family was living almost entirely on fish.

Stooping low, we crawled into the worn tent practically on our hands and knees. We were to see almost no other kind of habitation for a year and would become used to these postures. Many of the tents and sod dwellings called igloos are fitted with a door so tiny that the top of the door would come usually to my hips. This is not an architectural trait of ignorance, however; it is wisdom not to have a high or large doorway because in a land of relative fuel scarcity heat must be conserved, and the white man's door lets the household heat out every time the door is opened by folks going in and out.

Inside we blinked and could not see for a minute; room was made for us to sit cross-legged on the floor composed of a few packing-box boards, which Ruth, the daughter, swept with a gull's wing. A certain back rest was supplied the occupants by the fact that several caribou robes which composed the bedding were rolled back against the walls during the time the family was up and awake. As for the floor boards of these tents, these people move around to different locations quite a bit and would be found in their tent at different places during the year: when they move, their floor planking is left in the same spot for their return the following season. Although they may travel as far as a hundred and fifty miles to another location in some instances, the route is as commonplace to them as a morning's shopping route is to one of our housewives. A shopping route is what it is. All of the ground traversed is "home" to the Eskimos.

Connie and I removed our rubber boots from our suffering feet and spread our hands before the old burned-out sheet iron stove, huddling as close to it as we could get, while we shook from the chill of the sea. It has been said that a temperature of fifty degrees above zero when one is riding in an open boat on water is comparable in effect to a temperature of fifty degrees below zero when the water is frozen. The dampness had penetrated to our marrow. The Eskimo family, on the other hand, sat back away from the stove against the tent walls and it was noticeable that they kept their parkas on indoors. Later we found this to be entirely typical. They may wear their inner parkas with fur next to the skin almost all the time except when they are sleeping in other skins; it is necessary to wear such a parka all the year around beside the sea. Indoors and outdoors made little difference to them. A half dozen gnarled sticks were brought in by one of the children and thrown onto the floor beside the homemade stove. Summer or winter, among Eskimos the children usually get the sticks, unless, as in some camps, they must be brought long distances by dog sled. But one seldom sees more than these half dozen sticks ahead at a time! The half dozen sticks! How well we would know them! Just barely enough to keep the stove going, but somehow it goes, and the people just get by. A year in Eskimo land is enough to make any white person almost lose his mind unless he gets wise and stops worrying and learns to just get by himself when living with and dealing with Eskimos. Eskimos never worry, and they are usually the happiest people in the world. Why worry? The land here, when you get to know it, is not half as hostile as it looks; its bark is a good deal worse than its bite. It is actually a land flowing with milk and honey when you learn the few simple tricks of how to live in it. There is nothing to worry about. The seasonal life of wandering and hunting and fishing teaches primitive man to trust: he knows that Nature will provide, and, oddly enough, in every case except the one out of a million, she does. I could read Connie's civilized criticism as we visited and warmed ourselves, partaking of the hospitality of these tender creatures, the woman and her small children, residing alone on this hostile coast. I knew Connie was wondering how they would ever survive in this frail tent with the burned-out stove when the severe arctic winter came again. But somehow, they must have survived the winter before! The mere fact that they were here proved that! Look about! They were all extremely well, fat and vigorous, and appeared to be in ideal health. Their clothes were almost altogether skins, the family tent had several actual holes in it, burned by sparks from their smokestack, but the children's cheeks were as round and as red as great roses. This was especially true of the older daughter, Ruth. The women more than the men are remarkably fair, as they spend much time indoors and do not get tanned. Here, as we looked carefully at Ruth, was the first hint to us of the mixed blood along this coast.

"Do you like caribou meat?" Alice asked us, speaking for her brood.

"Yes, we certainly do."

Ruth of the blooming complexion, with her dark hair gleaming in neat braids, smiled and silently squatted on her square haunches to cut up some caribou heart and back fat in chunks into a pot of melting ice. She smiled but spoke no English. Alice presently interpreted to us that Ruth wanted to give Connie the beautiful new pair of sealskin house boots which the Eskimo girl was wearing. Thrilled by the offer, although the boots were too small for acceptance as a fit, Connie was won, and if a time should ever come when she could return the favor, she would particularly remember Ruth of Cyrus's house at Oliktok.

Connie went out to the canoe and got our tin plates, silver, and cups. She got a few handfuls of raisins from the meager five-pound supply which was supposed to last·us a year, and I gave Alice two .30-30 shells for Cyrus's rifle. It wasn't much but it was all we felt we could do at the time, considering the uncertainties of our own future along this unknown coast.

"I am sorry we have no salt," Alice told us, as Ruth served up the meat after it had boiled ten minutes. "We only caught one fox last winter, so we have no money to buy food from the trader." Alice explained that the family possessed but a few traps and that they could not catch many foxes, so that they did not have money to buy more traps. They owned only two small and very worn fish nets, so could not catch many fish—just enough to keep going day by day. Cyrus could not kill many caribou because the family could not afford many shells for his rifle. Consequently, their clothing was very poor. But one treasure Alice did possess at the time was a glass jar of coffee. Three things come first of all in modern Eskimo life, you see: these are coffee, tea, and tobacco.

Alice secured the coffee and opened it. Connie and I drank it when it was offered, and everybody, including the children, enjoyed this celebration. The coffee was black, unrelieved, of course, by any cream or sugar. Ruth neatly washed our dishes when we had finished.

We parted from the poverty-ridden family with a very warm feeling from their hospitality. That caribou meat was full of sand when your teeth ground down upon it, but it was offered in genuine kindness to a hungry stranger. Actually, it was stronger and better feed than we had been getting out of cans. Sand and all, it tasted pretty good.

We had been vaguely aware from childhood knowledge about the Eskimos that they eat a lot of sand in their food and that their teeth get worn down to the gums in old age from their chewing. This is true. We had not properly understood the condition before now, but soon realized that it is due to the fact that north Alaska is sandy, as are many arctic lands, and that it is very difficult to butcher meat in the summertime without getting sand rolled into it or blown into it by the restless coastal winds. Furthermore, as before mentioned, the Eskimos bury much of their meat in the ground from the summer hide hunting, and then pack it out by dogs, so that it takes little imagination to visualize the result in sand accumulation. They consider the sand inevitable and don't bother about it. They wear their teeth down not from chewing skins, as we had erroneously learned, but by eating sandy caribou meat. Yet there is somewhat of a miracle involved in this simple situation: it is the peculiar fact that no cavities in the teeth or tooth abscesses result from grinding the enamel off the teeth by sand. The Eskimos, and probably anybody else living in their environment, simply grow more ivory to replace that which is gone![1] This is believed due to the properties of their all-meat diet in some way.

We ourselves had a lot of faith in caribou meat. We looked forward eagerly to another year on it. I suppose people like us, who have "gone native" in a sense, would be regarded as in-betweens. We can find things to criticize about Eskimo life and do criticize it continuously, but we find many things likewise to criticize about the overly civilized and restricted life of our own people, too. One of the things we miss in civilization is our caribou meat.

At 11:05 P.M. we traveled onward from Oliktok. We said to Alice in parting: "We are going on to Beechey Point to night," to which she said, "My daughter Ruth, she says that she sees some ice over there, not far away." Somehow that remark given so casually in the soft musical Eskimo tones just went in one ear and out the other with us. We hardly noticed it in saying good-by. This brings up another general note on Eskimos: they will never tell you not to do anything you come out and propose to do, but will just let you go ahead.

We all waved, I pulled the starter rope with a flourish, and Connie and I were off again. Broad placid smiles faded away in the distance on the gravel spit which stuck out into the empty ocean behind us.

The greater polar sea lay like a glazed pavement ahead; it was fascinating to just travel on and on. What need had we ever to sleep while having an experience like this?

Around the corner, however, was the answer to that nagging doubt which had said in the beginning, "I'll stop you yet. Why, you can't canoe on the Arctic Ocean!"

What had we been expecting? A concrete answer to this query lay here in the form of a solid white line of ice which blocked the way ahead of us, stretching from shore, so it looked, straight out to the North Pole, blinking into the pink sky.

---

1   Vilhjalmur Stefansson, *Not by Bread Alone*.

"Well, I'll be doggoned! The ice pack!"

Like most people, we had read about the polar ice pack though we had never seen it before. But it's one of those things you know when you do see it. Perhaps we should have expected to meet some ice in the Arctic Ocean, for after all, that's what it's famous for. What was it like? We wanted to see it up close, even to touch it. Never fear, we would see plenty of it from now on, for it is no rarity here.

Could we find a way through it and past it to the next open water along the shore? As we drew up, we could see that it was merely composed of moving drifting cakes. There were even alleyways opening in between them. I thought we might get through, but Connie was on the conservative side about entering those alleyways; they closed in silently even as we looked. The ice was coming in now.

This was really only what is known as light bay ice, we later learned. The real polar pack stands outside the islands. The smooth bay ice of the lagoons is inconsequential to larger ships which are icebreakers and can ram the cakes, but the *Little Willow* was no icebreaker. Some of the ice blocks were the size of houses and stood four feet out of the water and of course weighed several tons. Even the little ones you couldn't move with your paddle; we tried it.

As we began to motor in and out between the silent ice cakes, Connie was nervous, but I wanted to make every inch of progress eastward along the shore that we could. "I think this is very foolish in our canvas canoe," Connie insisted, not unreasonably. But I was thinking of the coming winter, and I knew we must travel on a bit.

It was a lonesome hour in the night, about two in the morning, I think, when we were forced to camp at the end of what had been a very long day. As the arctic loons called and squaw ducks squabbled while they floated between the floating ice cakes about us, it came to us clearly that people along this ocean just don't depend on it for going anywhere much during the summer. Their traveling is mostly done by winter with the dog team. Some years there is no open season for ocean travel at all with boats. In the case of larger ships, anything much bigger than a canoe, one may wait weeks for one favorable day, all depending on the capricious ice pack, which moves in and out from the edge of the land at will.

This is why explorers, according to their accounts, always sledded in this country before we came along with a canoe. Their tales have dealt primarily with dog sleds and the winter season. Was it worth the trouble and the waiting around to try to see all of this coast by canoe? It would take two summers to do it: this summer, then a stay over the whole winter, and all of the next summer to reach our destination on Canada's Mackenzie. Yes, we thought that it was worth it. We wanted a new angle. Few white people now living have seen all of this coast by boat, and an ocean that is never seen when it is water is hardly an ocean at all. One is curious about it, to see every indentation of that coast and find out what it is like. We had plenty of time. This was our life and we were spending it happily just where we were, with new country to look forward to as each season turned. Yes, we would do it. We would see it all by canoe yet!

We had just time to reach the safety of land now before the ominous bay ice closed silently in. It came in like a ghost against the wind on an offshore breeze! This is one of the most curious facts about the movements of the ice; it has been authenticated long before our time by a number of observers. Strictly speaking, the wind is never directly from offshore, but the southwest wind and the northeast wind are the two prevailing winds at the top of our continent. The wind from the southwest brings in the ice on a certain tide at the same time it may bring up the inland mosquitoes clear to the edge of the water, so that the caribou may even swim to some of the islands to escape them. But the offshore breeze is a mild weather wind. It is feeble when it blows. The predominant wind is the blustering northeaster from the sea. It is fortunate that this wind can be depended upon for the most part, because then you know where you stand anyway. And as soon as it drops, the polar ice pack which has been held against the shore silently moves away. But against the wind the pack may move in on a lark, nobody quite knows why.

It was pink twilight when we pitched our tent on the oars and prepared for bed. To hold he canoe we would haul it up on land part way and stake it out with stakes driven into the mud. "Imagine us telling those Eskimos where we were going to go!" Connie laughed, as we struggled to pull the *Little Willow* further aground from the ice cakes which squeezed and popped against the shore. Soon there wasn't an inch of water left on the whole horizon.

"Do you suppose we'll be here the rest of the year?" "I don't know."
Our tent was raised within sight of Cyrus's camp down the shore.

The comings and goings of the polar ice pack before these people's front door meant little to them.

Cyrus's tent on the horizon was a welcome sight to strangers on this far shore where only the sea birds screamed and wheeled. The clouds which had veiled the sun these several hours diffused their pink light over the scene as they slowly changed their conformations in the sky which stretches over ancient Eskimo land.

5

For two days we camped on the bank of the ocean near Cyrus's tent at Oliktok, waiting for the ice to go away. Through the binoculars there seemed no end to it. But remember that we had but a two-to four-foot elevation from which to see. We could only dimly surmise the presence of the island reefs lying out to seaward—low sand and gravel ridges, lower even than we, built up by ice action and we could see nothing ahead.

I hunted around on the prairie with the .22 rifle and shot one of those big white snowy owls. These owls are numerous on the prairie by the sea, and you can have lots of fun chasing them, trying to stalk them by crawling up on your belly where there is no cover. The big white lazy owls are conspicuous against the summer grass; almost every two-foot knoll holds one, sticking up like a thumb. Snow owls have white meat like chicken and are very good eating when they are fat, but my hopes fell short when my summer owl proved to be but a skeleton with wings.

The driftwood I laboriously chopped refused to burn. It was my fault; I had tried to get dry wood from a big stump. This system had produced good wood in other climes, but it would not do here. Here one picks up very small drift, for it is dry and will burn, despite the fact that long years of drifting about in the polar ocean have sapped it of all its natural oils and resin. But those big soggy stumps are next to worthless.

"It almost looks like we're here to stay," we told ourselves with our usual adaptability, as we sat watching the pack press close and tight as the cakes grounded in the shallows. On the second day of our waiting the wind howled out of an arctic sky of cobalt blue. It blew right into the front flap of our tent, pressing the ice pack against the land. Of course, we had no idea that such a northeaster could be a good omen, that it went with a rise in tide which would lift the ice cakes off and take them away easily as soon as the wind dropped. "We just pinned up one of our two woolen blankets over the front of the tent with safety pins to break some of the wind, and hugged the small stove inside. We didn't have the right clothing for this environment. If we had known this before, how well we knew it now! No fabric clothing of the white man's conception of winter life can keep you warm in that cool breath of the polar ice, especially when the gale turns its blast around at you and comes right out of the North Pole, with nothing at all but thousands of miles of ice in between. A person can't keep warm in fabric clothing, not even in summer. That wind is right out of the icebox, the icebox of the world. We were just hanging on by our fingernails to the edge of Mother Nature's own great open icebox door.

Navigation on the Arctic Ocean is seldom possible at all until mid-July off Alaskan shores. It is rarely earlier than the last part of August, however, that any vessel can come around far northern, ice-locked Point Barrow, where the currents are particularly difficult, holding the whole polar pack against the shore at that spot. Therefore, in the old whaling days-and there were once half a hundred whaling ships in the Arctic Ocean in one season—a ship coming from San Francisco in the Pacific was usually outfitted for a three year voyage, inasmuch as it took the first year alone to merely work the ship by late August around Point Barrow and into the Arctic Ocean, where it must harbor and winter before it could begin its whaling on the second summer.

"Yes, we might be able to canoe on along this whole coast this one summer," we argued, "but on the other hand, we should know within two or three weeks from now just where we are going to live if we are going to winter on the arctic coast. We will have to hunt meat, have our clothing arranged for somehow, build our home before the sods are frozen, and gather driftwood for winter fuel. It would be different if we were going straight on and could make some civilized settlement our destination; we're not. We can't travel all summer and make winter preparations at the same time, can we?" Arctic explorers have typically found this true.

Having arrived at the Arctic Ocean we saw the truth of this last argument in no time at all. We could make a pretty good guess right now that summer in this part of the world lasts but a few weeks and might be called merely a lull, during which sledding is discontinued for a while in between seasons. Like all white men who have yet come down to the Eskimo coast, we had been obliged to sneak in by the grace of summer merely to make our preparations.

At four in the morning of the third day of being icebound, Connie awoke. It was not our hour to get up, but she explained that something woke her. The wind had dropped; that was it. Slipping from the sleeping bag she looked out the door of the tent and upon the circling sun which had never set. The Arctic Ocean before our tent lay like a pink pond in which myriads of wildfowl squabbled. The ice was gone!

The wail of the loons rose up again in a dirge, the heat pressed close from out of the continent, and our tent was full of mosquitoes whining in the sudden silence. All of these changes were recorded on Connie's subconscious mind until they finally wakened her out of sound sleep to seize upon an opportunity of importance.

"Up! Up!" she roused me, and within twenty minutes we had struck our camp and gone. We were free once more!

"We'd better hurry to make Beechey Point before the ice comes in again!"

The early morning sun hung like an ornament in the northeast, slightly veiled in drifting mists. I don't think that human being ever gazed upon more exotic scenes than those offered by the Arctic Ocean in summer to us in a canoe. The game today was fog! As we moved slowly and sleepily along the immense landscape of sea and sky, following the thin contour of the curving, mystical shore, the smell of smoke was wafted to us and soon the small flames of an open campfire attracted us ahead. Standing beside the fire at this hour in the morning were what we took at first to be two children. When we drew up, the doll-like figures with their tall ruffled hoods were really a full-grown man and young woman man and wife, as was later made clear. They and their drawn-up rowboat, their cooking fire with a coffeepot set on to boil, and the thoracic section of a caribou chopped squarely in two and thrown down bloodily on the sand beside them, stood out in simple relief with nothing else at all against the great backdrop of rolling cloud banks and storm streaked sky.

The man wore the first Eskimo water boots of hip length made of black sealskin which we had yet seen; he was dressed entirely in skins, his work clothes; they were battered and bloodstained. His name was Little Jacob and he was son-inlaw to Cyrus, married to Ruth's extremely good-looking younger sister, Carrie. But we were unable to learn at the time who this couple were because they spoke no English. Carrie was dressed in sky-blue calico over her furs, and her hood was of the white wolf, from under which smiled doe like olive eyes.

Considering the conditions, it being five in the morning at the top of the world with the rain beginning to fall upon all our heads, I kind of hoped for a handout when I saw that caribou, but they didn't ask us to stay, so we climbed back into our canoe and traveled on.

Soon we saw another camp. Here many people who had just gone to sleep piled out of their tents and awaited us by a beached whaleboat. About a ton of meat lay on a large ice cake which had been towed to shore and was held by a cast anchor beside their door. First glance attributed these disorderly piles of meat to the fact that the people had neglected to put the meat wherever they should put it. But wherever would that be? With the exception of the ice cellar plan, after all, what could be a better way to refrigerate and keep your ton of meat handy for household use than anchoring it on a cake of ice alongside?

By now the scene was getting familiar to us: tents pitched along the ocean front, a whaleboat or skiff pulled up nearby, people running back and forth on the spit or standing to greet us with their arms withdrawn from the loose sleeves of their parkas and folded across their chests; the smell of wood smoke drifting on the ocean; wild-looking dogs staked here and there; the skeletons of a few fish racks made of driftwood. The unrealness of it which struck our inland senses was the more sharp because the whole was superimposed upon such a vast and empty stage. The sea, the sky, and the prairie were so great as to nearly hide each tiny camp in their immensity. Against it all, as though they promenaded in some bleak, wind-swept theatrical scene, concocted to make a mood, were the people little doll-like figures almost as round as they were long, with the tall wild hoods of the wolf and wolverine, and multicolored snow shirts made of dyed flour sacks drawn over their caribou skin parkas, worn fur next to the skin.

These were Richard's People. Richard is a tall man about six feet with a heavy dark beard and the prominent nose of some seafaring

Englishman. He is brother to Alice and also to the old matriarch up the Colville, Matthew's wife; and all of the children encompassed within the family groups we have met are cousins to each other. As there are fifteen people in Matthew's group, ten people represented in Cyrus's group, and ten people in Richard's group, we had met families thus far representing thirty-five people.

As we shook hands, I noticed some black tarry-looking blimps lying on the ground all over the bank. Seals again. These are not fur seals such as the world hears about but hair seals of no value except to the Eskimo. No fur seals have ever been known to visit the Arctic Ocean that I know of except one, which the Eskimos told me they killed, and it must have been lost.

Richard's People are great for seals. The shiny surfaces and puffed-up sides of many spoke of oil stored within to be tapped as needed. Accouterments of every good Eskimo camp, seal oil pokes give off a spicy agreeable aroma, not bad if you are broad-minded. These hearty seal eaters had caught over one hundred foxes the previous winter and were wealthy by all the standards which mark this coast.

Connie wanted to know: "Are there big waves on this ocean?"

In carefully worded English, from one of the polite young women who had attended the Point Barrow school for a while, she learned," There are waves when the wind blows."

We were surrounded by human beings all along this coast, but we were finding that we were really alone, because of the vast differences in our points of view and the way our minds worked. The stranger among these people is traveling through what is their land still today, and it remains unseen by any but a very few of our own people who have wandered through it on occasion. At Richard's camp, for instance, if the stranger comes by and asks: "Is it five miles to Beechey Point?" the answer will be yes. A few minutes later, if he inquires again, to check his information, "It's about two miles to Beechey Point, isn't it?" the answer will again be yes. "Yes" and "I don't know" are the standard formulas for answering all questions, but never "No" to anything you propose to do. It isn't because anyone tries to deceive you; the people are often very willing to help but don't always understand yes from no. Therefore, they smile and give you the answer which they can see will please you. To get information from the Eskimos one must stop leisurely to chat and listen carefully to the topics which they bring up of their own accord, not suggesting any topic oneself, or that suggestion will be followed and elaborated upon with imagination. The politeness of the Oriental! The Eskimos are generally regarded as a very high type of primitive group who have come to our continent from Asia, probably since the fourth and last Glacial Period. Many of their attitudes and poses at times might be duplicates of what a person might see, we would suppose, in Tibet or old China.

Some of the people on this coast who have had several years of schooling at Barrow may understand your question about distances, but even the more educated may honestly not have the slightest idea how far a mile is. How could. they, when there isn't a mile marked out anyplace? We ourselves estimate it by lifelong experience. Yet many a person can't tell a mile from a few hundred yards, so how can we expect these other races to measure and advise about our travels in this scale?

In the distance small ice cakes could be seen floating as we left Richard's People. We pushed forward at a good clip, while loons dived and then appeared behind us or taxied off like a heavily loaded flying boat. Soon the sea took on that distanceless aspect it assumes when a gray fog blankets all. From shore I had seen a small lane through the ice before the fog descended.

For us the rest of the journey to Beechey Point was something between a bad dream and a comic opera. As I remarked: "Each mile you go along this coast you think you are going to round the point just ahead. But what you think is a point is really not. It's just where the land ahead stands out in mirage as it sinks below your vision around the curve of the earth."

Consequently, hour after hour, we approached each "point," but it was never the one we wanted. The coast line of the continent fell behind us and kept rising in front. Visibility from a small boat is certainly not over four or five miles on clear days because the land strip is so low. On this day we felt extremely cautious about getting far out from that low thin ribbon of the continent's edge that might so easily be lost.

It was necessary to make a detour out around some of this ice to proceed at all from Richard's camp; five-foot bay ice of the previous year was moving very slowly as we commenced weaving in and out among the cakes with our busily churning motor. Just a mile out to sea there was apparently endless open water; if we could just get out to that we could travel outside the whole thing. This, incidentally, was the mistake the Karluk made.

Beechey Point curved out to sea, we knew, and I didn't think we could miss it. A bold course, but this fog hung just over the floating ice, and we might as well try to go out and get into the clear and make a run for it.

But oh, running outside the ice is guaranteed to age a person a hundred years! The lanes we followed between the floating cakes were as complex as a maze as we wove in figure S's. Sometimes I stopped the motor altogether, in some blind alley so as to turn around and with our paddles back out. Rafts of a hundred old squaw ducks then all laughed at us as loudly as they could. Sometimes they dotted the sides of the big green pans like lumps of coal. We found they aren't helpless either, just because they can't fly during molting, for they can swim and dive like a seal.

"Where's land?" I asked presently, and Connie pointed straight out to sea! It was indeed remarkable, I thought myself, as I looked in the direction she pointed, how exactly a low strip of clouds over the ice cakes out that way did counterfeit land. I didn't like this.

I got out my pocket compass. Shoreline was where I had thought it was, all right, but its two to four-foot elevation was barely perceptible in the mist; if one didn't know land was there, he could easily miss the whole continent. "That there's the shore line," I informed Connie bluntly. "Now don't take your eye off it a minute and I'll navigate the boat."

Connie's head whirled around like an owl's while I wove around and around through the ice lanes. The sameness of sea and sky, and those ghostlike ice cakes herding about us, made it seem that an eternity of time had passed before we got to that lane of open water which we had almost given up finding, because we knew, too, that the ice was moving and changing all the time. But going back to shore the way we had come out seemed equally hazardous, kind of the way an egg probably feels in a rock crusher.

The open water enabled us at last to proceed full speed ahead, paralleling the faint line of the continent's edge. The ice slackened out entirely, once we had left the bays, and the sea was silver smooth. No time was to be lost. The fog lifted here, and we thought we saw definitely a connection between the land strip we were following and what we had taken for an island on our left. This island now moved around in front. We saw that the continent curved out to sea then, in gentle undulations, in the shape of a half-moon; on the end of the last curve, we calculated, should by all means lie Beechey Point.

Pointing the bow of the canoe straight out, we headed for one of the farther promontories. It seemed to have houses on it. "What do you make of it, Bud?"

With the glasses, I replied, "Well, if they're houses, they are all made of mud. But I suppose you could expect that." Abruptly the promontories moved right into the water as we pulled near! They were not miles away; they were right here! We found ourselves grounding on a beach and the houses turned out to be mud banks with a two-foot elevation above the sea. Where on earth were we?

In the fog we had perhaps missed the mainland, then, and might have been following a chain of islands all this time; perhaps we had motored far off our course to end up on an island of the Arctic Ocean. Would we be able to get back to the mainland again?

When I climbed up the embankment with the binoculars, the firm ground under my tottering legs held no sign of occupancy by human beings, while the cold sea washed nearby. What time was it? It was two in the afternoon and we had been going since four in the morning, and no breakfast yet! In my bones were misgivings. "Darn those Eskimos," I thought. "They know we are strangers here and we try to get information, but do you think they'll tell us anything? Not a word, if they saw us heading straight out for the North Pole." I am sure almost everyone has at times had thoughts similar to these who has ever been in a position where he has had to depend upon natives for help.

"But you see," the opposition countered in my brain, "they take it for granted that we know all this. What white men they have ever seen have been great white men. They have led them to expect miracles, so that they never doubt for a minute that if you propose to do something you will do it. They may not even consider that we are subject to the same dangers they are. Yes, so often I have seen it with the Indians of the forest regions who think of white people as subject to a different set of rules altogether and from their own exigencies set apart."

Another step over the rise! This wasn't an island! We had been right in the first place. We had run into a little cape on the mainland which curved out. Beechey Point was the point yet ahead. This time two large frame houses, with a cluster of little white tents blooming about them, could really be seen. There could be no mistake, although from here the whole thing looked as though it sat in the ocean.

Headed at last for what was truly Beechey Point out in the sea, we were passing through the suburbs just an hour later: white tents of Eskimo families gleaming on the green prairie, flanking ice-jammed coves and bays. We did not go into these bays to call, but purred straight ahead across the smooth open sea for the tall buildings. The tall reflection of the two big houses walked along as we progressed, and still retreated. We could sense that on the shore Eskimos were listening now to the unfamiliar sound of an outboard motor coming out of the fog along the quiet ocean toward them and into their lives.

Now we could see that Beechey Point's two large houses were each really a string of buildings attached together. The smaller group of joined-together buildings stood apart from the big barn. Their layout looked for all the world like a prairie farm in Nebraska or Kansas, where only the smaller structures are actually used by people for living. The architecture was the same, even to the big frame buildings covered with sheet iron to break the wind, and the small buildings, for pioneer life, banked with sod.

When we drew near, two men came walking from the big barn down to the beach. One was plainly an old Eskimo man Samuel. The other was a long-legged lynx-faced man in the prime of his late thirties who might have been some good actor made up as Hollywood's conception of a halfbreed. His name was Abraham, and he was the manager of the Beechey Point branch of the Barrow Native Store, which is the Eskimos' own adventure into business. Abraham lived in a tent out on the Jones Islands most of his life until three years ago when he took up residence in the big house here. He figures up the books and gets fifty dollars a month for his living wage, except that if he traps foxes this winter his wage will be reduced during the time, he is absent from the post.

Connie and I will tell of the Eskimos with all of their faults as well as all of their virtues. They are just a real, very human people, and all of them are different individuals. Indian Service and missionaries interpret them according to their own views, but it seems to us they need somebody from the outside who would be a completely unbiased interpreter. They are our oldest as well as our newest Americans, about whom the rest of us have many myths and false impressions. Eskimos live in the most hostile environment which is known to support human beings. Yet it is a richer environment nutritionally than the land of the Indians below; and the great plains of our north beyond timber line, because they are grazing grounds, may yet prove more valuable than all of Alaska's much esteemed forest!

There is nothing here but prairie and sky to look at, by the side of the polar sea. Yet to anyone with vision, whom the river has hurried at last from the enclosed shelter of the dark green spruce forests of the interior out upon the sprawling plains of that distant beyond, ancient Eskimo land, with its scattering of countless caribou bones and its fallen sod mounds and tent rings of prehistoric towns, becomes the campsites of the Dakotas.

The Arctic Ocean bounds the burial grounds of mammoth that foraged 50,000 years ago not long at that! Only a thousand miles straight out your front door is the North Pole, perhaps to become a main highway of commerce.

A few white men have liked this view so much that they have settled in arctic lands to stay. Thus, we have the development of the so-called "Eskimoized white man," a unique species. The charm of the arctic lies in many things. For us right now, we look out to that polar sea each day, and it gives us a kind of funny feeling of just hanging onto the edge of great things. There is little known about that primeval ocean at all. Here is something so gigantic in nature that all other things described by naturalists pale beside it. Man has not yet bent this to his will.

Yet there has been a civilization of human beings living here around the polar coasts of the world from time back into antiquity. They are nice people, a gentle race.

When I am far away, I shall remember our Eskimos of Beechey Point. I shall never again be able to forget the Arctic Ocean when it lay like a pink millpond on summer evenings, when we set our nets just outside the door and the floats would bob with the great load of fish. Nor can I ever forget the openness of the prairie life; I shall ever, think kindly of winds and fog. I can't forget the voices of the winds of the top of the world that I learned to love.

By summer's prairie lakes and Iceland poppies, and the ever-present blink of white ice to seaward; by winter's yellow lantern light, and drifting snows and shadows etched on friendly Eskimo features, and hands dipped deeply into the seal oil, I shall think of this land. And

The Colville River

I suppose a strange lump will come in my throat and many times for no reason at all there will come before me again in the night the vision of that bleak old barn of a trading post, Beechey Point, standing all by itself these years beside the sea, bringing back the year that Connie and I took off from civilization to spend with the Eskimos there.

Abraham and Dora at Beechey Point

George Woods's tent

PART THREE

Beechey Point

Connie with George Woods

Martha Woods

1

At Beechey Point balls of white foam were rolling along the shore, borne by the wind. Our teeth were chattering from our cold ride on the Arctic Ocean, but the two Eskimo men who greeted us on the beach stood conversing with us for several minutes before asking us if we would care to come up to the big house and inside. They had no conception of how long we had waited and shivered to get here to what we regarded as a shelter. Of course, we couldn't know then the vast; gulf between the psychology of a people who are used to looking at the world from out the windows of their houses who merely exist from house to house as it were and the psychology of a people who possess no houses at all but are used to living all their lives out of doors. Along the coast of the Arctic Ocean it did not occur to the Eskimos that we were looking for houses or that we were cold.

When we did gain admittance into the Beechey Point trading post, this gaunt structure which rears out of the sea for miles on the skyline offered little of what could be called warmth by any terms. We followed our guides through several dreary bare rooms, closing doors behind us. This dwelling, although solidly built, could never be heated thoroughly, even in summer, and any persons who resided here must inhabit only the back room as actual living quarters. This was, in fact, the usual arrangement. The plan of the white man's arctic dwelling is that one should enter the actual living quarters through a series of compartments, so that the changes will be gradual. Ernest de K. Leffingwell, explorer who lived along this coast mapping it during the years 1906-1919, suggests in papers for the United States Government "that one should enter first a shed, then an outer room, then a short passageway into the house proper. The shed may consist of an open framework covered with canvas here the dogs may sleep and be fed, and wood be cut up for the stoves the outer room may be built of driftwood or boards sodded over, or banked with snow in winter. It is used for storage of material which is not damaged by freezing and which must be kept away from the dogs. Firewood, ice for drinking water, barrels of provisions, and dog food are kept there. A workshop should be sufficiently long for the construction or repair of sleds."[1] This well presents the picture of arctic life as it has always been lived up to the present time.

As we passed shivering through the outer sheds and rooms of the old Beechey Point post we saw piles of dead ptarmigan, ducks, brant, loons, and gulls, thrown in heaps upon the chilled floor. They were partly for human food and partly for dogs, and had been lying here, some of them, for a month, as the Eskimos and a good many arctic white men enjoy their fish and meat eaten "high" as well as fresh. Two of the familiar black seal-oil pokes lay on the floor of the outer room also, but it seemed strange to see them inside a house. These pokes are made by skinning a seal through its mouth to obtain the skin for a bag. The word "poke" means bag in Eskimo and is one of the Eskimo words, like "igloo," which we have unconsciously adopted into our own language through the Alaskan gold seekers who fell into the habit of speaking of a poke of gold dust. To make the poke the seal is skinned as we would turn a sock; the flippers are cut off at the first joint, the natural body openings are tied up, and chunks of raw seal blubber or whale blubber are stuffed tightly inside. The top is tied then, and the whole thing left to lie for a few months to a year. The oil dries out and ferments inside the airtight bag. When some oil is wanted for household use a flipper is cut off, forming a spout or spigot.

In the workshop an old Eskimo, Mr. Lynd, sat making his family a new stove out of an empty oil barrel as we passed. In the following

---

1 *The Canning River Region of Northern Alaska* by Ernest de K. Leffingwell. Professional Paper 109, U. S. Geological Survey under Department of the Interior. Government Printing Office, Washington, D. C., 1919.

room, almost empty, an Eskimo drum hung from a coat hanger, while a shotgun and several white fox skins filled the remaining hooks.

The last room, the high-ceilinged and paneled kitchen, was full of Eskimos when we entered. They were all dressed in their best snow shirts over their parkas, with smiling shy faces showing from within great wolf-trimmed hoods. They sat on the cold wooden floor along the walls, where bare cupboards supported a few china dishes and a young woman in a print house dress stuffed a few miserable sticks into a feebly burning old-style wood range. She gave it up presently and started up a primus stove.

Connie and I were asked to sit on straight kitchen chairs at a table and were served hot coffee with condensed milk and sugar by several attractive young women in fancy mukluks and house dresses of bright colors. If a woman wore a light washable house dress only, the dress was always what we would call many sizes too large, due to the fact that Eskimos like their clothing to fit loose, as a parka does, and often enough the long woolen underwear beneath showed from short sleeves or down the legs to be tucked into cotton stockings. The men wore work pants and work shirts, which could be seen if they took their parkas off. But as we have said, parkas are often worn indoors here as well as outdoors. Connie and I plunged into the food, hungrily eating down strips of raw dried caribou back fat and slices of homemade bread, never knowing that we were eating, too, the only bowl of sugar and the only can of milk with our coffee that existed on the entire north coast of North America. These people had offered their best.

"The girls are bashful," said Abraham, while the beaming maidens giggled and blushed. Suddenly all the female attention was drawn to an object outside the window. We wondered what it was that could so take their interest. Abraham walked to the window and explained, "They see a ground squirrel." These people are hunters, and the girls were quick to spy out anything that moved on the prairie any time of day.

Abraham, son of a white whaler and an Eskimo mother, could speak English quite well, but later we realized that he did not understand many of those things we took it for granted that he did, and that many of his agreeable nods when he listened to us expound might signify nothing at all except politeness.

First, we learned that the Beechey Point trading post was out of everything and that we could buy nothing. There was no salt, not even a nail to be had. "I guess they forget all about us over at Barrow," Abraham said. "No boat with grub now for two years. This is the second summer we are waiting now for some food and calico."

Right away the thought came into my mind that Abraham wanted to buy things from us, if he could, and that I would probably let him have a little for his own use, as a gift of course, until the boat came with food, provided we decided to settle here. But to supply a whole coast hereabouts with the few things that a fourteen-foot canoe can carry would be quite a task if it came to that. The arctic coast, Abraham said, was all out of ammunition, too. All were waiting for the yearly supply ship, the North Star, to round the corner to Barrow. First, Barrow's population must be served, and then whatever was left over or whatever they happened to give us would be shuttled eastward our way, provided the fall freeze up had not by then closed the ocean.

We asked about the distribution of Eskimos on the coast and about the presence of people to the eastward towards Canada. We learned that there is a similar native trading post at Barter Island, serving approximately the same number of people as around here, but since Barter Island gets its goods in turn only from Beechey Point, it was worse off than this place for supplies of any sort. What about fuel? Abraham remarked it was a long way by canoe, he thought, to reach a winter location beyond Beechey Point where there would be either suitable drift for fuel or people living. Abraham was cagey. He didn't know exactly who we were or what we were doing here at first, but he was feeling his way towards the possibility of our staying around because he knew that the presence of the right kind of white people will bring money and prosperity into an Eskimo community, not to mention the diversion and the entertainment that such an occasion might make. As I looked at him, I realized that the slanted folds of skin over his eyes gave Abraham a shrewd look, and yet we shouldn't judge anybody for looks that he can't help. The glittering eye and slanted lid combined with a figure around six feet tall to make Abraham quite a handsome person in a way which seemed to match the appearance of this country from which he had sprung.

Hours must have passed as we talked. Old Samuel, kindly old fellow, got out his cheap portable phonograph and we heard, "Has Anybody Seen My Lovin' Henry?" and the "Homebrew Rag," which was on the other side of that record; then it was time to eat again. The patrons

Beechey Point

of Beechey Point who come into the dreary old arctic house on state occasions most frequently sit upon the floor for their entertainment, and this we all did now at a legless table of boards laid upon the floor before us by a handsome girl named Dora.

If many of these people surrounding Connie and I were not of pure Eskimo blood, no unsuspecting stranger would have guessed this fact. A person who didn't know any better would describe himself as being among "real Eskimos." It is true that here we were with some of the realest Eskimos living now in the world. These are actually today's arctic Eskimos in their own costumes, and it was the Eskimo language which was spoken entirely about us. No one would suspect that a generation ago this ocean was filled with the world's greatest whaling fleet, and San Francisco adventurers and traders. Those days have come and gone. All is swallowed up in the arctic. Yet for all that, the arctic always has produced a very cosmopolitan society. Today therefore there flourishes here on our northern shores a unique culture all its own as the result: the culture of the twentieth-century Eskimo of larger stature and longer limbs than the first explorers saw and of fairer skin probably than even twenty-five years ago, rapidly turning white! This Eskimo is anxious to partake of the things of the modem world, so far as he can obtain them by any means in his land, and he has a portable phonograph and a seal-oil poke lying side by side where he camps in the house, arctic style.

Sitting on the floor of the house with the others, Connie and I smiled at each other as Presbyterian grace was dutifully pronounced in the Eskimo language over food upon china plates: dried caribou meat, held in hand, which everybody cut with his hunting knife by the side of his mouth as he chewed, and, on individual salad dishes, some year-old fermented seal oil to dip the meat in. The oil is a kind of salad or dressing. It is sometimes called "Eskimo butter," Abraham explained. I can enjoy it when I am hungry, I learned, but I have always remained conscious of the fact that seal oil, whale oil, and the uncooked oils of sea animals contain an element in them which sticks like paint if you try to use them for polishing your stove, and out of which, in fact, house paint can be made. Maybe that's the Vitamin D coming off, but it is usually considered too powerful for the stomach to take unless you are in practice, and there seems some truth in this; as much as a tablespoonful of it is an explosive, volatile, raw body fuel. Eskimos and habituated whites use it with discretion and moderation. As a native arctic food, it should probably be encouraged for all.

The dessert course consisted of straight tea and bread. Square, heavy-set children, packed on the backs of their mothers underneath the parka, with heads sticking out beside the mothers' heads, chewed a piece of meat and then squirmed around to the front under the parka to get at the breast; each one pushed and pulled and sometimes beat upon the patient mother, until presently you might see only two contented chubby feet sticking out from her dress, clad in sealskin booties.

The dried meat we all ate was not like the long-dried meat of last winter which Connie and I had brought with us in the *Little Willow*. This meat had been sun-dried for merely a week in sides of ribs hung on beams from the roof of the trading post. The drying sun and wind had formed a protective casement over the outside of it which kept the meat from spoiling and sealed the juices within. Starved as we were, with sea appetites, we found the Eskimo sun-dried meat to be delicious, despite the fact that the Eskimos had not picked all the caribou hairs off it. After a year already spent in arctic regions, living off the country, Connie and I had reached the point where we were surprised at nothing and repelled by little. Perhaps it is what has been termed "the wisdom of the body" which was taking care of us in a different climate, under uncivilized conditions where we had to forage on our own. But one must live, and it takes a highly civilized person, we contend, to be intelligent enough to realize just this.

Aboriginal diet is the tediously learned wisdom of trial and error passed down from countless generations in getting along best in a certain locality. Populations survive during the vast time elapse by slow migration. Historically, no single lifetime or series of lifetimes is long enough to actually observe these migrations caused by nutrition or the search for food; they must be deduced. The primitive Eskimo, as an illustration, knows by long tradition that his diet is best for his locale. The white man is duped if he thinks that he can improve upon it. It was difficult for the white men here to convince the first Eskimos, a short time ago, that flour and sugar are edible. All of these people around Connie and me in this generation, while they cried for flour and sugar, still felt they could never give up eating meat in their old traditional ways, and it was meat, not bread, which was the staff of life to them.

Many educators, physicians, scientists, and missionaries with wide experience would say that this, in fact, is exactly why Beechey Point people, cursed with a lack of sugar and flour, are in ratio blessed with abundant health while living almost solely on their native fish and meat. The white man who comes to their land to stay for long, if he is without the fresh fruits and vegetables and the sunlight he is used to in his own land, had best do as the Eskimos do and live on meat too; he has to.

Of course, Connie and I did not have time to think of all these things then; we were just adaptable and had our eyes open to try anything once. It was a whole year later that word reached Connie, coming from a friend who is an elderly medical scientist, which confirmed the course of action we had taken. "The explorer," said this man, "can subsist for a time but not for generations unless he conforms. This matter of conforming is something for you and Bud to think about. Always remember that latitude and environment were there first, and will so continue within human memory."

How did the Eskimos come to this big house which was not of their building? Gradually we were to learn that a succession of white traders had lived here at different times during the past fifty years. Last and most recent of these was Jack Smith a name typical of the men of lonely lands. He was a prospector and trader in the Koyukuk originally. We had heard of him over there and were prepared to say a hello from friends if we found him. From Abraham we pieced out Jack Smith's story. It seems that late in life he got tired of being so settled down over there on the Koyukuk and so he pulled out for the arctic coast. First, he went up some river into the Brooks Range. He connected with one of the head rivers of the Colville and came down it years before we got this idea ourselves. There are names of two explorers in geological journals to date who have done this Howard (of Howard Pass) and Schrader and conceivably there are some others with whom you wouldn't be acquainted offhand, but it does make you wonder about the Jack Smiths, who never are in journals. Jack was alone, and he had a twenty-foot flat-bottomed river boat and no motor. Just what he lived on most people would find hard to say, unless they learned to know the Brooks Range as that old man must have known it. It took him three years to make the trip. Spewed out of the Colville mouth into the Arctic Ocean, Jack Smith turned to the eastward, just as naturally as we did. He found Beechey Point and this old trading post, then run by another old arctic man. One wonders if he shivered the same way we did that first day he arrived. He bought out the trader then in residence for a few thousand in pocket cash, married Abraham's young stepdaughter, then seventeen years old, and in his mid-seventies became the undisputed father of three children of his own and patron saint of an all-Eskimo community.

I imagine old Jack really loved life. One of his hobbies was cooking and baking for the Eskimos and giving them parties. It is said that an immense horde lived at his table. He imported fresh eggs in a barrel, and such things as oranges and apples with his fleet of cargo boats from Point Barrow. Then, for something to do, he decided to take up sealing, and according to the Eskimos he became an expert sealer and often put up more seals than anybody else in the spring. The seals were used for dog food and of course they had, and have, a value of around five dollars each. Old Jack was bald on top, and he was left-handed when he whittled on a stick of wood. It took me a year to learn these details from the Eskimos about a person I have never seen and from whose china dishes we ate this first day. The Eskimos observed every smallest detail carefully about his life and daily habits, and once when Connie's Ruth of Oliktok, Connie's later companion, did a drawing for us of the scene of Fourth of July at Beechey Point as she remembered it, there was Jack Smith in the distance of the picture while the Eskimos danced in the midnight sun, old Jack Smith being recognized by long overcoat and a handbag, as the single white man just walking into the borderline of Eskimo consciousness.

Jack used to get his winter fuel by boat trip each summer up the Colville River to those veins of coal we saw. He too had recognized them for what they are. It was when he was on one of these trips for coal just three summers before we came along that he died. He had had heart trouble for a long time. The mourning crew of his friends brought him to Beechey Point, and they have never been for coal since, either. Beside the trading post just outside the window Jack Smith sleeps now on the prairie, buried by the Eskimos.

After Jack's death the Eskimos decided to buy up the interests and take the place over themselves in the name of the Barrow Native Store with which they and their relatives are all affiliated. Jack's widow took the children and departed by plane from Barrow to make her residence in one of the larger cities of Alaska.

When Abraham, the store manager, who alone of these people could speak English, learned that we were harmless enough, his nerves relaxed, and he became very kind. He was a chain smoker and at first had jittered and twitched continuously. Becoming more used to us in time, our new friend, moody, strange, never completely understood, sent us onward with a big sack of Dora's freshly baked bread, some window glass, and some borrowed traps. We had decided to settle nearby for the year and had asked the whereabouts of the entrance into the ocean of the nearest sizable creek or river because we wanted to have easy access by canoe inland to the hunting and freighting out of caribou; Abraham directed us, therefore, six miles on eastward from Beechey Point to the entrance of a river called the Kuparuk. Yes, we had found the kind of Eskimo community we wanted, and we were willing to call it a day. Having had enough of trying to make our canoe be an icebreaker along an almost totally uninhabited coast line of hostile nature we were finished with shivering around without the right clothing and finished with taking chances.

The next thing now was to put in our order for some Eskimo clothes. We must have our measurements taken by an Eskimo seamstress. Abraham commended us to the ministrations of the household of George and Nanny Woods, who became our Eskimo mother and father and to whom we became big children that they loved.

Loading our canoe with driftwood

We begin building a sod house on the Kuparuk River delta

2

In a little lagoon, safe from the buffeting of the sea, we made our canoe safe just a half mile down the beach. This was the camp of George Woods. He is a Kobuk Eskimo of mixed strains who left Alatna and Wiseman on the Koyukuk River years ago to come over the divide by way of the John River and Anaktuvuk sled pass. Raised in a Koyukuk mining camp and exposed to the ways of white men in his early boyhood, George Woods could speak better English than Abraham, perhaps. His family spoke no English, but as we crouched to enter the tent beneath the lowering storm clouds which hung over our backs, his wife, we thought, could just then be heard telling the children to "scram." She had picked up a few words of English.

George said, as we relaxed gratefully in the warm camp stove glow, "You see, we are just common folks here. It's just an old Eskimo camp, but make yourself at home. I just came over here a few years ago myself on a trip, but I got married and got stuck here."

Asked if he liked this country as well as the forest, this likable fellow with the sense of humor said: "It's too cold. The first year I shiver so my teeth, they rattle. The next year I learn how to take care of myself. But a man here, he has to have good woman to sew. I get married to have her. You have to have the right clothing, that's the thing to get along here. But I never did learn how to be a seal hunter."

Asked later if he would like to have his picture taken with the family kayak, the inland Eskimo demurred, as would any of us, saying: "But please don't ask me to get in it. I would tip over."

George's wife Nanny, whose Eskimo name is Oinjak, meaning "Open Waters," had busied herself making tea as soon as we arrived. Tea and hard biscuits are as inevitable to the modern Eskimo camp as air so long as the people have anything at all. Nanny's biscuits were hard naturally because she had only water to mix with the flour, as is so often the case. Yet like Abraham's Dora, she was an excellent baker when she had the ingredients; many Eskimo women can bake superb bread which it would be hard to beat anywhere. All the family grouped in a circle on the floor boards of the tent, grace was said, and we grabbed. As there were some dozen pairs of hands grabbing, the biscuits disappeared fast. Next came fish which had been cut into chunks and cooked with their scales, fins, and heads left on. They were served by placing the big pan of fish in the center of the floor while all crouched and ate with their fingers from the central pot except Connie and I, who had brought our own plates. Connie served me up a fish head for my first portion to have her little joke. I ate around the eyes and made haste to reach for another piece of my own choosing. Do not civilized people prize cheeks of halibut on the hotel menu? The Eskimos prize the same thing, only it is whitefish and is served with less ceremony. Also. among the fish were a few sea trout of a delicate pink flesh and very delicious. All the fish had been baked in the oven in a monstrous frying pan. All we ever saw the Eskimos use a frying pan for, incidentally, was for baking, as it has never occurred to them to fry meats; they do not know what a steak is or if they do know they repudiate fried foods a very reasonable adjustment which the human being of all races makes if he is living on meat and fish eaten three times a day. Within a few minutes about fifteen pounds of fresh fish had vanished, leaving only skeletons. Dinner was over.

After the refreshments Nanny took our measurements for the new clothing which she agreed to make us. The negotiations took some hours. The family laughed a great deal about the amount of skins it would take to make me a parka. We learned that approximately sixteen caribou skins would be needed to equip Connie and me in full Eskimo dress according to the proper styles for man and woman and the numbers of changes which are needed on the trail for much traveling and in this life, one never knows when he will be called upon to travel.

Many people would find this large number of skins hard to believe, and even to us it sounded incredible at first. We had thought that one could wrap a caribou skin around himself and have skin to spare, and that that was about all there is to it. If the uninformed imagine this, they are all wrong. A deer's skin with its long slim legs is so small when it is tanned that you wonder how the deer originally fitted into it. No part of the hide at all is wasted, either, in making Eskimo clothing. The legs of the skin are of immense value, incidentally, for they are just about the only material of which good winter boots can be made. It takes two deer or eight legs to make one pair of boots for a person. The head skin of the deer is used to make the hood of the parka, with the slits of the eyes sewed up and some inserts of white belly hair, according to the dictates of Eskimo fashion.

The whole principle of the warm, windproof Eskimo deerskin clothing is at the same time its very roominess and loose fit; this factor takes more skins than the inexperienced would allow for. The person who is encased in it is something of a walking tent; the light weight of the robes and their fluffiness make the clothing not uncomfortable by any means, while the texture of the caribou hair itself against your skin is soft as plush upholstery. However, it does take an enormous number of summer-killed skins to have the right clothing, which must be made once each year if worn steadily by a resident of the arctic I don't mean dressy clothing, particularly, but what is worn for everyday arctic life and work. This is the kind of clothing that the Eskimos wear themselves. It is expensive as well as luxurious in its way. Any kind of arctic clothing yet devised by us is more so. It would cost us, as it costs these people when it is figured out, about $300 in all for our year's clothing here, and more if we expected to have any extra for souvenirs or display. The cost would be somewhat less, depending on how many skins we ourselves supplied toward our own clothing. The Eskimos were busy hunting for themselves and it did not seem likely that they would hunt for us. We would have to bring our own skins in. Prime hides for clothing sold for five to seven dollars each at this time A fawn skin brings around eight dollars, untanned.

One young boy, age twenty-one, George Woods's oldest living son, called Apiak, with the son of another family, was at this very time out hunting on the prairie for the skins which must supply the entire winter clothing of a joint group of thirteen people, mostly women and children, dependent on him. Young hunters were scarce at this time on this coast, with an immense number of dependents for each hunter to support.

One person's clothing requirements are as follows, generally speaking:

        Inner parka - 2 skins
        Outer parka - 2 skins
        Fur stockings - 1 skin
        Two pairs fur pants - 2 skins
        Mittens and boot soles -1 skin
        Total - 8 skins

These skins would include two pairs of boots from the legs. A new sleeping bag should be made each year if caribou is used, and a certain amount of miscellaneous bedding and tent flooring will be made from old bulls and winterkilled caribou whose hair is long. Connie and I were fortunate to be the only white people we know of today to wear the real Eskimo clothing of north Alaska. This clothing, like the oldtime costume of the Navajos, may be a museum piece within the next few years.

Some will say that we did wrong to live as the Eskimos do. They could say that living by hunting is the inherited right of these people because they are primitive aborigines who belong here while we do not. But times are changing. As we have shown, an Eskimo has first to be defined. The people who actually live here as Eskimos originate in all the seven seas. And as for being primitive, the boy Apiak who was out hunting skins for his family now was using exactly the same make of rifle as I. This was a .30-30 carbine. People who live in the arctic, aside from armies and government personnel supported outside, are placed pretty much on a par where survival is concerned.

What about reindeer for food and parkas? There is an impression that our Alaska Eskimos are living on herded reindeer. That reindeer are needed for food and parkas is true enough, but that they supply these items in Alaska to any extent at all is not true. In 1938 Beechey Point had four thousand deer and now didn't have one for the reason that the people would not consistently take care of the deer in which they had invested. Correspondingly, the wild caribou herds seemed to have increased at about the same time, according to the Eskimos, for in the period of 1938 to 1946 there were plenty of animals which could be hunted.

Beechey Point

At the time we arrived at Beechey Point, therefore, there were no domestic reindeer at all and we depended during 1945-1946 entirely on the wild American herds for our food and clothing.

In connection with Eskimo clothing, Connie and I learned that there are certain unalterable styles for men and certain other styles for women and that fashion dictates these in Eskimo land. The clothing and customs which we quote here are of course for just the part of the arctic over which the United States has jurisdiction; other Eskimos in the different lands have slightly different modes of existence and varying customs. The clothing here we found has been modified in the last twenty-five years from the original, and style today with both sexes takes precedence over comfort or is tending to. A strong point in illustration is that women travel out on the dog-sled trail wearing only cotton women's stockings of the kind which can be bought at any of our department stores above their caribou skin boot tops, and they have no leg covering as they used to have. Since Connie wore long woolen underwear and woolen pants for household wear underneath her parka, the combination was not too bad except in severe weather on the longer trips. But she really needed fur pants, too, which she never did get. Another change in Eskimo garb is found in the outer parkas of the men, which used to come down almost to the knees in a long "dress" effect. These have gradually been shortened to our mail-order catalogue's conception of a popular sportsman's jacket. These changes we consider undesirable since the climate has not changed and they detract from comfort.

The trimming on parkas remains conspicuous as it doubtless always was, as nearly as we can tell, and this is a most important aspect in Eskimo dress. The women today usually use much more fancywork on their clothing than do the men, however, and there is great rivalry among the young belles in the matter of parka trim. The woman's hood must have a little pouch hanging down in the nape of the neck, making its cut different from the hood of the man's parka, and we have suggested to the people that this may have originated from the fact that a baby's head is often found sticking from that place, but no one seems to know today the origin of this style. The woman must have a trimming to her hood of either wolf fringe or wolverine or both, the more elaborate and the longer the hair, the better. Women affect a tall wolf hood made only of the mane and cape of the wolf, which is expensive and difficult to obtain, but lasts a lifetime. There seems to be a belief among our own people in Alaska, and it is often written in northern books, that wolverine is the only fur which can be used to trim the parka hood because it is the only hair which won't frost up from the exhalations of the breath. This is not true. All furs will frost up, but the frost can be beaten off either wolf or wolverine without serious abuse because these are exceptionally durable furs. Big ruffs around the face to trim the parka are very desirable, one often hears essential, to break the wind from the cheeks, but a main reason for their use is the matter of dressing in the right style if you can.

"White hair inserted in the right places on the man's outer parka to alternate with the dark brown of the usual caribou hair is important in the world of fashion; the white is always scarce and in high demand, because it is found natively only on a part of the caribou's belly. The conspicuously marked domestic reindeer skins of imported herds should suit Eskimo taste for fancy dress where such skins are available, but the Eskimos complain that domesticated reindeer skins are heavier for wearing and they do not like them so well. Throughout most of more settled Alaska to the southward much white calfskin for fancy trim is imported from the United States for the Indians and Eskimos to purchase. At Hughes on the Koyukuk, black and white spotted Belgian hares raised domestically for market in the United States bring from the Indians $1.75 the skin.

Fawnskins are very highly prized by the northern Eskimos on the prairies for their lightness and durability, especially by those young hunters who run ahead of the sled all day long. The Eskimos conspire in early summer to kill great numbers of these newborn fawns, or they may kill the cow caribou to get the skin of the unborn fawns. Dogs get most of the fawn carcasses. Caribou killed after September purely for food have hair too long to manage for clothing unless it is sheared by scissors, as is sometimes done in emergency, but this makes the hair ends scratchy and prickly, and only children or very old people are seen to wear clothing made of such skins. The Eskimos leave hundreds of hides on the butchering grounds at other seasons than late summer, which are never used, except for the legs; these winter hides make good bedding and there is no reason why anybody should sleep cold on this coast. Yet many do sleep cold of nights because of these people's unexplainable negligence—the greatest fault of the Eskimo character.

One can explain it in part only by stating simply that negligence and improvidence are the characteristics of the amiable, aimless primitive. No Eskimo ever worries about next winter or next week. All Eskimos would rather go cold or let their children go cold than wear sheared skins if they do not get enough summer skins that year. Connie and I had wanted to live among the most primitive and isolated American aborigines today, and we had asked for it. We know now that the Eskimos of north Alaska are a great deal more advanced, for all that, than certain Indian groups found on reservations in the United States, which we had left years before in the quest for the strange.

Our measurements for clothing were taken by Nanny's expert eye in a glance; a little pinching here and there to see how fat we were soon cleared up any doubts. My inner parka and fall wading boots must come first, as I was the main support of our family; Connie would have to wait longer for hers. The result was that we both waited for a time.

In connection with wearing Eskimo clothing and living in the arctic the question frequently asked is how one takes a bath and how he keeps his clothes clean. We shall dispose of this question at once so as to make the picture as clear as we can. Fur clothing of course cannot be washed; when it is worn out after a year it is simply thrown away. What one does wash in a basin with soap and water is the light set of underclothes and light socks he will be wise to wear next the skin; these take relatively little water for washing in a land where water is hard to get in the wintertime.

It is difficult to teach the white man how to wear native clothing because it is possible to ruin a set of clothing in a week. One must be careful not to run one's boots over; if skin clothing becomes wet it must be dried slowly-not hung by the stove. The care which skin clothing requires is one of the main difficulties in its ever becoming practical for armies or large groups of men, as they would have to be individually trained to its use. As regards cleanliness, in the arctic we learn to be more careful than is the week-end camper who spatters his clothing with pancake batter or tears it off him in the woods. We can't afford to treat our clothing roughly. Actually, there is nothing to get it dirty after the snow comes. The furs keep clean, and inside the house, where we are dressed in our usual woolen work shirts and pants, we need wash them only once or twice in a year if we take care. One gets dirtier in a single week end's trip in the dust and sand of southerly lands than he does in half a year here! Your face can go unwashed for weeks in the wintertime and show barely a trace of grime. The body does not perspire at the rate it does in a temperate land, while the porousness of caribou skins helps towards ventilation in a way which fabric clothing insulated with down or made of domestic sheep (the most practical white man's substitute found so far) cannot do. The person living in Eskimo clothing learns to control his perspiration on the trail by shedding a layer as soon as he starts to get hot, because he knows that perspiration causes dangerous complications which must be avoided in the arctic. He will take a bath and a rubdown in a basin once in a while and that disposes of the question of baths. It sounds bad. but our ancestors only recently knew nothing different!

We said good-by to the Woods family and headed out to sea once more, bucking the rolling waves. It was around eight o'clock in the morning of a new day. We had not found time to sleep in some thirty hours, for the nocturnal Eskimos enjoyed entertaining all night. That's the way things go in the primitive life, where opportunities are seasonal and every thing happens at once when it does happen.

Now we were tired out and visibility over the ocean was poor, but we must find the place where we would pitch our tent and sleep some miles away at the mouth of the Kuparuk River. On and on stretched the same dim strip of shore line, rounding the curve of the earth before us and dropping from sight behind, while we battled up mountains of waves and down. Beechey Point and lynx-faced Abraham, the trader, and George and Nanny Woods and the fitting for our new Eskimo clothing might have been a dream except that what seemed hours later we heard carefree singing and met a group of young hunters and children with their pack dogs. They were trooping along the shore on their return from a hunt twenty-five miles away. Yes, children not over the age of eleven, boys and girls together, dressed all in caribou, were singing and shouting on their way as carefree as you please, beside the foggy sea through dew-sprinkled wildflowers, with packs of bloody skins on their backs.

Seeing these children made us ashamed that we had begun to grow alarmed over finding the missing Kuparuk River. We found it eventually. Its delta was about three miles broad and we had to investigate each channel and cubbyhole in the cold dripping fog, hardly knowing whether we were still on this earth or in the afterworld.

Finding a river mouth in fog and waves along an indented shore line of very low terrain is no simple matter. With numb fingers that could hardly accomplish their task we managed to pitch our tent upon the spot where we thought the Kuparuk River must be. It later proved to be but a bay leading by devious channels into the Kuparuk. We drank the Arctic Ocean for three days and didn't know it. You see it is not hard to make this mistake because the large amount of melted ice and the water pouring off the land keeps this ocean in summer rather drinkable, although prolonged drinking of it will cause diarrhea.

"Say," I called to Connie on the third day, as we labored at our new home site, "you can stop hauling those buckets of water a quarter of a mile up the bay just to drink. We're just drinking the Arctic Ocean all the time anyway. There's a seepage of it into the ponds, too." We had learned one reason why the Eskimos drink melted ice.

We camp on an ice floe containing fresh water

Bud's first ugrug

3

How we worked on that house we were going to build for our winter's home, Connie scouring the beaches for driftwood supports, and I cutting and laying the sods! In the evening of the third day our house all fell down, and we were disgusted. So much for the first house.

After that we moved the tent down along the beach from the mouth of the Kuparuk River to where a better winter view would be offered on the seacoast. We got our water from ponds inland. Here we might see the ice pack all winter long from our front window, we thought. Most of the first day here passed in unloading the canoe once more and making piles of our goods on the shore. Then we went across to an island in the Kuparuk delta to get a better choice of wood. The short trip is indicative of our daily perils perhaps. The canoe was so buoyant emptied of its load that it charged the waves like a bucking horse; then the wind blew our only paddle overboard. Our other paddle was on the mainland holding up the tent. Around and around we circled and at last grabbed the paddle from the trough of the waves. At the island we made some piles of wood and decided we would bring the canoe around on the other side to load. At this point the island neck was so narrow that we would have been wise, I know now, to have lifted the canoe bodily across. Flowers were blooming on the island and the sun shone above. Leaving my alpaca-lined and hooded winter coat, the only one I had thus far, upon our woodpile, as well as the precious ax and saw,

I commenced to motor us around the island. But the strip of low land went on interminably. We got stuck in the mud in the shallows of the delta and waves rolled into the canoe. Then with alarming suddenness a fog borne by a violent wind swept in from the sea and blotted all out. It was with difficulty that we were able to recognize where we were and get our wood and clothing and tools at all, after a several hours' run among the mud bars. So much for a short trip! Later that evening we could hear the sound of Eskimos singing—some ancient chant out somewhere on the ocean from a boat, the sounds of a safe, happy, and prospering people borne on a balmy breeze. Was this land tame or was it wild? Do children sing where explorers perish? We couldn't decide. We would have to obtain more evidence. It was the next day that our thermometer registered eighty-four degrees in the sun and sixty-eight degrees in the shade, our hottest coastal day. The lapping wavelets of the sea were the color of turquoise; eider ducks with orange bills drifted by. The Iceland poppies and anemones fringed the beach in their full glory of color while Connie crouched at the edge of the sea washing dishes in hip boots with her mosquito head net pulled down. We worked happily at building house number two. I found a blue Russian trade bead. How on earth did that get here?

The following day the temperature sank to thirty-three degrees and it drizzled all day. I put in a full day at house building, dressed in rubber hip boots and slicker, and at intervals when the rain halted, I donned mosquito head net against the rising swarms of attackers. Connie stayed indoors, only emerging at intervals to give her strength to a driftwood beam or to make a quick skirmish of the shore for an extra bundle of chips and rubbish to burn. She had killed three ptarmigan and we fed well on these, what with pancakes and canned butter and the last of the strawberry jam. We had both tea and powdered milk to drink.

The driftwood was heavy as iron from sogginess and was difficult to burn. Smaller pieces were of all shapes, so gnarled and crooked that fitting them into the camp stove was an art in itself. I estimated that one canoe load of drift gathered from this locality was equal to one week of fuel for winter; about forty canoe loads must be gathered, at the rate of perhaps three a day. Of course, we were rich compared to all these other human beings along this ocean. We had a motor to take us everywhere. How did the Eskimos get their winter's fuel?

The winds and wet wood of the arctic coast! In contrast to the timbered interior Alaska that we were used to, a windless day here was rare. We must have felt that same homesickness and that lost feeling that all white people feel who first come down to the polar basin. The wind would blow, and then it would turn around and blow itself back the other way again, restlessly, ceaselessly—and that's the whole story of arctic coastal climate throughout the year. The wind caused us trouble with the stove smoking in the tent. Now the in-landers could be seen hanging the stove around five times to cook a meal. Finally, I had to cut a new hole for the stovepipe in the roof of the tent and sew up the back hole, setting up exactly as the natives do.

One day while I worked, Connie took a cautious five-hour hunt inland on the prairie looking for caribou and using my compass. She saw many things—little Lapland longspurs, arctic loons with their single offspring floating on a lake, wildflowers, a red fox which she crept up on in a cross wind where he was curled up at the end of a mound. The fox's bed was woolly from shedding hair which hung from him in yellow tatters as he went loping away; she brought me home a handful of it in her pocket. Walking across chains of little lakes she reported that you sink down in soft mud and then hit solid bottom where it remains frozen underneath. It rained periodically, and Connie walked in yellow fields of sunlight dappled by blue-black water and waving prairie grasses and blue-black sky over which a full rainbow spread. For a minute, she said, she felt as though she had almost got hold of the mythical pot of gold which is said to lie at the foot of that rainbow. So, it had been here all the time, on this farthest prairie in the breath of this polar sea, with big white icebergs tipped on end and blinking just out there beyond, and we guessed the world had never realized this before. When Connie got back, she found me worried about the house caving in before I could get the roof on to hold the leaning walls. The walls were built about two feet thick out of sods weighing altogether several tons. The inside dimensions of it were seven by nine feet at the floor and it was a little over six feet high. Of course, neither of us had ever seen a sod house before, since they can't be seen in our generation, but we knew the early Americans in the prairie states used to build them. We could only do our best. I think I would have got onto it had I continued trying long enough. Generally speaking, I had found so far that playing with mud pies out in the summer arctic rain at a temperature of just one degree above freezing is not the best sort of occupation I can think of, and more than ever I had come to admire those early Americans.

The day we "moved in" was rainy. I crawled into the dismal structure, fearful that the whole thing would collapse upon me, while Connie stood by with the shovel. One by one I removed the props. A ticklish moment—and the house stood by itself. But we could not summon up the courage to sleep inside it. We kept wondering when it was going to fall. What a home was our little old sod shanty! The water had seeped up from the earth when the sod layer was removed and was four inches deep upon the floor inside, while the mud walls themselves fairly exuded dampness. "Of course, we'll have to run the stove full blast in here for some time to dry it out," I told Connie with an attempt at bravado. "Sod houses are always this way when they are first built." But I never could seriously convince even myself that we would ever live in it. Again, we learned for ourselves why the Eskimos do things a certain way. They live in their tents by summer at least, with all reason. The tents are dry; sod houses leak. Originally. they used tents of skins which were oiled; now they use tents which they sew to their own specifications on their sewing machines, from traders' canvas.

I suggested then what Connie had been thinking about all the time while I played with my mud pies: that we move to Beechey Point with the intention of wintering there right in the village itself. We could reside either in one of the two little sod houses already built beside the trading post perhaps, or perhaps in another house of our own building, with help. "After all, we are here to study the Eskimos," we said, keeping our own egos intact, "and there will be much closer contact with them if we live right at Beechey Point."

"Yes, and we'll just go hunting for a few days for a change from this housebuilding, and we'll freight a good load of meat back to Beechey Point while we're over this way," we said.

With the thermometer hanging at freezing and the rain misting down in fine droplets, we started out to find caribou. There were no more smoky stoves or mud pies anyway now; we left the stove behind. We figured there wouldn't be enough fuel inland up the Kuparuk River to fill it. We would have to weather it out with a cold tent as we had done before at times and with the down sleeping bag. A cooking fire could be built with a few twigs in a hole in the river bank. "When we get some fresh meat to eat, we'll soon be cheered up," we decided, quite abruptly, diagnosing our own medicine.

It is amazing how difficult it may be to discover a route inland when there are water channels leading in every possible direction and, but one channel can be the correct one. A day passed in just getting into the unexplored river.

We had only a little rice and tea. All our provisions were going fast. We were jaded with canned and dried foods, so that we just disgustedly left them behind, depending on our own prowess to succeed in hunting. Knowing the dread tales of scurvy to come out of the arctic, no person can help but be extraordinarily careful in this environment; it is not possible to eat too much meat, since it is the only food which supplies any vitamins at all which you can trust here, yet it supplies all of them in abundance when used plentifully. We had been three weeks with only occasional snatches at fish, and our spirits were not good, our digestions were upset, and our gums sore from the richness of condensed foods. Food concentrates like straight pancakes and bacon and jam have killed many a white man in the North, and this is no exaggeration.

Stomach ulcers have historically been common with such men as the Hudson's Bay Company men in Canada, who used to live on bacon and beans. But Eskimos living on meat only have never had stomach trouble. If this view of the situation seems contradictory to the reader in view of the tales, he has formerly read of white men starving or sickening on a diet of meat in the wilderness, then he must be prepared for a reversal of his beliefs and realize that all of these years his head, like most other people's, has probably been filled with superstitious old wives' tales.

For instance, Ernest Thompson Seton, the famous naturalist, writes of one incident in his book *The Arctic Prairies*:

> Our diet consisted of nothing but moose meat and tea; we had neither sugar nor salt, and the craving for farinaceous food was strong and growing. We were what the natives call "flour hungry"; our 3-times-a-day prospect of Moose, Moose, Moose, was becoming loathsome.[1]

---

1 Ernest Thompson Seton, *The Arctic Prairies*. Charles Scribner's Sons, New

Yes, I know that over and over again we read these tales, many of them from reputable sources. From the early adventurers to the modern ones we hear that when forced to subsist on meat they feared for their health and even for their lives. Even the natives of today think they cannot live without white man's food in most places in the world. But is this not merely psychological with the natives, because we have trained them in this way? Connie and I knew that we could live entirely on meat very well, because we had done it, but the trick lies in knowing how to choose it for butchering and then how to use it after you have got it. Simply cutting a steak off an animal is not it; there are other things to eat from an animal besides roasts and steaks.

The second day up the Kuparuk River was perfect hunting weather, cloudless, cool, and exhilarating. No mosquitoes would we see again after August 4. The Kuparuk River we found to be much like the Colville and its sprawling channels, and in fact like all those rivers which run off the arctic slope of Alaska in that it soon becomes shallow with riffles as one goes inland, and a motor is of but part-time use; soon we were out pushing and lining over the shallow rocky bottom, until the river would deepen again on the next curve and the motor could be used once more though with some hazard. On such a river, the use of dogs for tracking a boat is much handier than the modern motor. Connie pulled the canoe in her hip boots while I would hunt the bluffs and the prairie a mile or two inland. Parka squirrels shot in the head and dumped into the canoe bow would go along with us until caribou were found. The old boar squirrels smelled like skunks and we hoped we wouldn't have to eat them. Connie shot several of them with the .22 rifle the first few miles to get a supply ahead, just in case. Their fur is a burnt-orange color and is worth 25 cents at the trading post, not because they are worth that much, but because the more congested Point Barrow Eskimos are desperate to buy any kind of fur from our crowd at all out of which a parka can be made. On her excursions, during which I took my spells at pulling the canoe, Connie brought me two gifts. One gift was the foot of a giant rabbit. She found it in a gully. It had the hair and claws on it and was pure white and so immense that it seemed as though it should have come off an antelope. After examining it, we threw it away, and this was too bad

---

York, 1911.

because when we told our tale to Abraham at Beechey Point, he stated positively that there are no rabbits of any kind here and none of the Eskimos hereabouts have ever seen a rabbit in their lives or run across such evidence. No doubt Connie had happened upon the remains of what is known as the arctic hare, but we had only read of them in books before. Never numerous in nature, they may be almost extinct on this continent.

Connie's second gift was a handful of small red things which had been growing on a vine on the ground and which appeared to be berries. But if berries, they were bitter, for she had eaten half a dozen of them. Opening a "berry" carefully with my penknife, I derived a certain amusement in proving to her that it was a formation resulting from an infection of the plant by a parasite. Each red blister was just full of tiny crawling worms. Ugh! Poor Connie ran for the river to wash her mouth out, but it was too late then. She shouldn't have been so greedy for berries.

There are some cranberries and blueberries to be found on the arctic slope, but Beechey Point is almost as far north as land goes on our continent and no berries grow near there. We were to see no berries this year.

The immense gravel bars of the clear-water Kuparuk bore evidence of the big floods of springtime. The gravel was so clean and uniform that it could have been sold as Number 1 grade anywhere. Snow flurries surrounded us at times while flowers bloomed heedlessly. now-capped peaks of mountains which we believed to be the Sadlerochits, the Shubliks, and the Franklins rose in a front many miles to the south and east. These are part of the twelve mountain groups which are held to compose the Brooks Range and some of which are known to possess small glaciers—a most unusual phenomenon in the arctic; none of these glaciers reach the sea. No human being has ever set foot in most of these different mountain groups.

Caribou hair was washed up in a fluffy band along the edges of the pure river, showing that the caribou must be thick on their natural range. But the cold wind was depressing to us who were without parkas, and all of the caribou tracks were a week or more old. There are jokes of course about the man who starts out to track a caribou down. You see caribou frequently walk fifty miles in a day, and think nothing of it. On the fourth day, still not having eaten a parka squirrel, we made camp near 3 P.M. The country looked likely; I had seen two fresh caribou tracks only a few hours old. We left our tent, each with a carbine packed on the back with a buckskin thong, hunting in opposite directions. Connie returned to camp after a five-hour hunt, and sat watching a simmering pot which contained a solitary cock ptarmigan. She stole a glance at the carcasses of parka squirrels which still lay untouched in the bottom of the canoe, but made no move to get them out.

It was about 10 P.M., seven hours later, and I had progressed some eight miles up the river in my wandering circuit when I saw two caribou feeding two miles away from me on the prairie. They were across a lake from me which was a mile wide. I circled the lake and lay down in the path which the caribou were traveling.

I have since heard hunters say that caribou are one of the easiest and most stupid of animals to kill. I beg to disagree. Since this book deals largely with caribou and with life as lived on caribou, I will say here that this may be so when the animals are on migration to the southward, as seen by the average white man, but is not so when the caribou are found in their natural home. This was my first experience in hunting on the prairie, and I had to teach myself.

I found that there is nothing whatsoever to hide behind on the arctic prairie when stalking caribou for food and clothing which we had to have. How is one to get close to them? Later I was to be constantly within sight of as many as 10,000 to 20,000 caribou without being able to get one to eat for several days. This first encounter is a typical instance of summer hunting. As there was nothing to hide behind, I made no attempt to hide. The prairie hunter must lie still and wait for his animals to come to him. At six hundred yards away, the caribou could not see me because their eyes are not that good, but I should have to be on guard that they did not scent me. To have crouched in order to make myself smaller might have seemed the reasonable thing to do from the view of the inexperienced, who might hope to creep close in this way, but the caribou would have taken me for a wolf and bolted in that case. I just lay down flat on my stomach and trusted to blend into the scenery, although I felt far from being a blend. I had heard of this kind of hunting before but was trying it out for the first time myself. Would it really work? Yes, animals do not seem to recognize a danger in a motionless object. A cat doesn't attempt to hide when it waits for a mouse, and neither did I.

The caribou fed onward until they were perhaps three hundred yards away. But there they lay down to rest! Like two domestic animals they lounged there. I looked through the telescope sight I had mounted on my rifle for just this contingency and felt that I could easily hit one animal. Still, we were badly in need of them both. When a man hunts for his food and his winter's parka, he isn't likely to mess up a hunt by shooting from too far. And so, I lay, while clouds gathered, and snow began to fall softly all around. The leisurely caribou moved twice, only to lie down again.

Two more hours had dragged past by the time the deer decided to resume their grazing. When they got up, they fed off at an angle, changing their direction. When I realized they were never going to come any closer to me than they were then, I shot one at probably one hundred yards. He lay down quietly-a paunch shot, far back which was what I wanted him to do. He would be quiet, and he would never get up. The other caribou never even looked up but kept on eating. I reloaded and shot him too. This time I held for his heart and hit. Away he dashed. Two hundred yards he made it, and then he tumbled end over end, stone dead. But had the first caribou been shot through the heart like that he would probably have alarmed the other and I would have lost the second caribou. Paunch-shooting caribou is an old Eskimo trick. I had learned that the year before for certain emergencies.

Both were young bulls of about 225 pounds. I had wanted very old bulls for eating, since they are the fattest, but I had wanted cows and fawns for skins, so I compromised on young bulls. These young bull skins made Connie's parka and were almost as lightweight as cow skins would have been. The young bulls were in good shape, too, showing a little fat.

Snow fell heavily as I dressed the animals and hid the meat under the skins in hopes the jaegers and bulls would not get at it before we could pack out. I was tired and empty after a night of it, and realized one doesn't have much poop, so to speak, when he doesn't have good meat to eat steadily. I would be darned lucky if I could find my way back to our tent through this snowstorm without getting lost.

The walk back proved to be a long one. A small white tent on a winding prairie river, not all of whose windings you are too sure of in the first place, is a hard mark to hit across ten miles of lake-dotted prairie that is white in itself. I knew what direction the river and tent were even if there were no landmarks in this kind of navigation. But the clumsy hip boots chafed my feet raw over the ups and downs, and I was shaking with cold. Keeping the wind at the same angle on my cheek, I made a line for it. If I missed, I knew I would hit the river above the tent and so could follow it down to camp. I allowed to miss the tent on purpose for this reason. Luck was with me, and at eight the next morning I saw the tent as the storm lifted. I had been gone on this hunt since three the previous afternoon and had come out well from my first prairie assignment.

Connie had grown worried when I was out all night, especially when the snow flurry struck. She had just crawled into the bag to get warm, and in front of the tent she had a pot of rice and ptarmigan kept hot in the earth for me. She was not too surprised, but was very delighted when I pulled two long caribou tongues out of my pockets. The sight sent her rocketing out of bed to gather dead willow twigs for fuel, since boiled caribou tongue is about the most prized delicacy that a northern prairie hunter can get hold of. We had eaten caribou tongue before now.

After a few hours' sleep the tongues were cooked and we devoured them; then we broke camp and moved on upriver to work at the caribou kill. We got the canoe within two miles of the kill, and packed out one animal that day. But by the time we could get to the second one a day later, the gulls, jaegers, and foxes had ripped the hide badly, and the heart, liver, and head had completely disappeared as though they had never been, while big holes had been pecked in the quarters of the meat everywhere, besides much evidence that birds had just perched on it and used it for a general roosting place. We carried out what we could clean up and redeem. An inch of wet snow dampened the ground but melted as the sun circled.

In hunting for food, we never cut the meat off the bones to leave the bones lying in the field as many city hunters unfortunately do in the belief that they are discarding waste and avoiding a heavy pack. We have found the bones to be the most flavorsome parts of the animal when one is living entirely or largely on straight meat. Therefore, we took pains to gather up all the lower leg bones for boiling with other parts of the meat-for they would impart flavor! Our first breakfast after we got meat to camp was boiled brisket with the hot soup to drink, native style, and how we had missed it! Brisket is a favorite arctic food, as it was with the old buffalo hunters. We hadn't had any such food for two months or since last May, when winter hunting had ended for us. After three or four fat meals of choice items, we found ourselves gaining immediate strength and spirits, not to mention an appetite. My own lagging zest for food was so increased that I could consume extra bowls of rice, at which I had turned up my nose before. Thus, starvation rations now became a dessert to add the last touch to a feast.

Having had enough caribou hunting to satisfy us, considering that we didn't have the right clothing and were cold all of the time except when we were in the sleeping bag, we were heading right now for Beechey Point and Nanny, our seamstress. Perhaps she had already started a parka from skins which Apiak might have brought in. I hoped so!

I hate to think about that trip out from our hunting grounds to the ocean again. We calculated with optimism that the forty-mile run out to the Kuparuk mouth should be done in five hours downstream, and we would be by our warm stove again and thawed out. But the motor broke several shear pins on the rocks when we tried to navigate that wretched river. Our light canvas gloves were wet; our feet in the rubber hip boots were equally so in the freezing fogs. At intervals when we got out to pull the boat and thrash along through the rolling waves, we could scarcely walk for stiffness. We could hardly speak either for chattering teeth, so that our predicament must have been something like George Woods's first year. Our socks were worn out from the year before. The elbows of all our shirts had worn out, and the truth of it was that we had not afforded to buy new ones. Connie hadn't combed her hair in days, but would just tie her parka jacket hood tight about her face as she crawled from bed each morning, and so would remain all day until she crawled into the sack again at the day's end; losing the last of her bobby pins out hunting caribou was almost the final jolt to feminine morale.

Now as we neared the Kuparuk mouth, the fog closed in on us and we found ourselves drifting down a part of the Kuparuk delta and did not know how to get out of it. As the wind from the sea coming into the mouth of the river was so violent, we dared not go farther, but must go back up the river and hunt the other small channel through the delta by which we had entered originally. This exhausted our patience. Blown up on mud bars in a tearing wind, wet with icy spray, unable to run the little kicker in the shallows, we fought with enfeebled paddles to get off again. Finally, a sickness in the pit of the stomach, caused by exposure and exhaustion, made us give up the absurd idea of reaching home that night. At midnight we camped, stove less, lost in the delta of the Kuparuk River, probably two miles from our mud home by air.

It was that evening that in a spurt of anger I dug into a wave with my paddle and broke the damn paddle in two.

Some months later Abraham at Beechey Point, a few miles away, remarked of some of our Eskimos: "They thought they hear some people shouting over there one time."

We explained quickly, "Oh, that must have been us. You know we were singing." Abraham nodded in satisfaction.

After twelve hours in the bag we awoke to find visibility unimproved in the Kuparuk delta. You could see about one half mile and that half mile held no familiar landmarks. We hated to get up. A northern camper should never stint on the cost of his sleeping bag. If he gets around much with it, it will save his life sometime. We had not eaten in twenty-four hours. There was no wood. We started back up the river again, with our heavy boatload of chilled caribou meat and our almost refrigerated selves, looking for the channel we must have missed somewhere in coming down. The wind on our backs from the open sea blew our canoe along in mountainous combers. Trying to discern the saltiness of the water by taste was no solution to where we were. Presently we came back to where we had camped. Facing the wind now, we determined to go out around the delta then by sea, a wet course for the person in the bow, a nerve-rending course for both, and possibly—the saints forbid!—a suicidal course for the adventurous. A breakfast of hot water and steaks roasted over a bonfire derived from a God-given pile of drift, and we were fortified. The bonfire was built in a hollow among some of the most beautiful wildflowers we had yet seen; bent to the force of the wind, the flowers were not nearly as cold as we, to judge by the looks of them. They were surviving freezing temperatures and then some! The hardiness of arctic flowers is amazing. But it is mostly the wind which makes the difference in the extent human beings feel cold. We stayed by the fire a couple of hours in a state of semi-comfort, I suppose you would call it, burning drift, dreading to make the actual decision to face the sea, wondering if we would be alive two hours hence. No wonder these native Eskimo people have developed a character which fits their land and their mode of life exactly! Connie and I didn't profit by the example of these earlier adapted people around us. We hadn't got a parka yet. We fought the elements instead of abiding them.

Out we went into the sea, which grew even shallower with mud bars as we progressed. It was 7 P.M. again, a whole day had passed, and we had not progressed four miles from where we had camped the night before. Fretting at delay as we thought of these wasted weeks of fleeting summer and of our winter housing as yet undecided and no woodpile in, we knew thankfulness just to be safe for the moment and to have a boatload of caribou meat-precious cargo.

It was too dangerous. We returned to the same spot, erected the tent, and went to sleep once more. Early arctic explorers have written of going to bed to get warm and of how the gradual warmth of the bag sends one into a very spasm of uncontrolled shaking as he commences to thaw out. And so, with us.

At four-thirty the next morning the wild sea had calmed. This would be the quietest time in the entire twenty-four hours in all likelihood. We anticipated a rising wind with day. By six we struck camp and pushed out on the ocean once more, taking our chances of slipping across the front of the Kuparuk delta safely. It was necessary to make a long detour out into the ocean in order to cross the front of the delta. Anxiously our eyes scanned the horizon; the familiar fog banks rolled near at hand. How glad we were at last to see that tiny mound of mud rising out of the sea and to identify it with the glasses s our house! The trip was made in two hours with the motor.

At home we wolfed fried meat and pancakes, and soaked our blue feet in a bucket of hot water. I shaved, and I tied a mosquito head net on Connie's hair in an attractive manner to hold it in place for an appearance among the respectable Eskimos. Connie felt happier. The sea remaining calm, we reached Beechey Point in a few hours, had two heavy meals, one at George Woods's camp cooked by Nanny, and one inside the big trading post with Abraham. I made a second trip back to our mud house on the Kuparuk then to get the remainder of our load that same day, while Connie went to sleep with the Woods family in their tent. Abraham and his girl Dora accompanied me on my trip; they wanted to go for the ride!

As Nanny and George accepted the skins we brought to make our clothing and Abraham lowered our meat into the ice cellar at Beechey Point with a slant-eyed smile, I wondered if they could imagine just what we had gone through during these intervening days. If the Eskimos imagined, they did not show it in any way, and we did not inform them.

When Abraham told us we could rent Jack Smith's own little house beside the trading post for a small monthly sum-it had curtains at the windows and a linoleum floor and nobody living there at all!— we thought that the problem of our winter's habitation was solved by Providence in a remarkable way after all. Without any regrets we abandoned the little mud house at the mouth of the Kuparuk which we had never lived in.

It is still there, a landmark on arctic shores where there are almost no other landmarks made by man in a thousand miles of Eskimo coast line. You'll see it, if you ever get over that way.

4

The house which was to be our headquarters the year in the Beechey Point vicinity had been built in sections. First came a dog shed. Driftwood was used for a framework over which canvas strips of varying shapes and kinds were nailed. The roof was of corrugated sheet iron. Here I chopped our wood in cold weather. Here, too, one could store up a quantity of fuel if he could get it ahead. It was smelly place, with untold buckets standing full of ashes, empty cans and jars, old bones which had been flung out the door of the living quarters, dead gulls. Numberless fox skulls could be kicked about among the wood chips on its floor, showing how many a fox carcass had at various times supplied dog feed here for the fox trappers. Among this debris, lying on the floor of the shed, Connie found the scattered and dismembered parts of an old ice cream freezer. It belonged to Abraham now and had been passed down from the era of Jack Smith; it could make ice cream provided a person ever possessed ingredients.

The dog shed ran into a sheet-iron shed supplied with outdoor cabinets or an icebox of sorts for keeping fish and birds handy for the house. At this point, you opened a door, covered on the outside with caribou skin, and entered the living quarters. There was a back room which was also included in the living quarters, which Abraham had built, white man style, himself, but knowing from the first that we couldn't well heat it, we closed it early in the fall and used it mainly thereafter for a storeroom, hanging a canvas up over the doorless doorway, since we didn't have a door.

The color scheme of our living room was cream and green, and the whole was very attractive indoors. There was a really nice kitchen table, and stools and chairs. There was a Sears, Roebuck wood cooking range in modern design of a cream color enamel. The many-paned large windows on either side in this well-built house were of four thicknesses of glass between us and the outdoors. For arctic habitation, windows are not usually made to open and do not ventilate. The ventilator was in the roof, a built-in tunnel which could be opened or closed in the ceiling by a sliding panel. Ventilation is extremely important in the arctic, due to the dangers of carbon monoxide poisoning from stoves. There is a special tendency for people to enclose themselves in small places so that the dangers of carbon monoxide must constantly be guarded against. The Eskimos may not have a word for carbon monoxide poisoning in their language, but they do seem to know that ventilation is of importance, for every Eskimo igloo has a large ventilator as an accommodation for the crowds of people whom they entertain in a small space. The outside of our house was of clapboards, and when we first moved in there were three polar bear hides swinging alongside on a high clothesline, bleaching in the powerful northern sun, while the turquoise wavelets of the sea danced before. The outside of the house was an array of packing-box boards and heavy tar paper, and it had a heavy, sod-covered roof. On the box boards which had been used in construction were written many names: CASTEL-now that would be Aarnout, of Banks Island fame; PETERSON-that would be old Peter Peterson of the great arctic whaling annals who knew this ocean and kept his own secrets, as they all did in those days. Both of these once were traders at Beechey Point and lived in this house. WILKINS-now that would be Sir Hubert of the Explorers' Club, who else? A famous name in polar exploration, as anybody knows. Abraham knew him. Leffingwell the geographer's name was also on one of the packing-case house boards, holding the tar paper onto our house. A snapshot of Charles and Anne Lindbergh hung on an interior wall, taken by one of the Eskimos when the fliers stopped over at Point Barrow on their way "North to the Orient." How could we be lonely with such a distinguished company of adventurers?

As soon as we moved in, I began to talk to Abraham about the fuel situation. He informed me that every good stick had been picked up for miles around, and that wood was generally hauled for the village in summer by the Native Store cargo boat, except that the cargo boat was at Point Barrow now. I encouraged Abraham to make a wood-getting expedition with the post's whaleboat, using my kicker for power. The whaleboat hadn't been launched this summer yet, but about twenty of us, mostly the village women, managed to launch her and rig her up. She leaked badly but with constant bailing we could float her. It was one of those blue and gold days of idyllic beauty on sea and shore which Beechey Point can expect to see but a few times in the whole year. It corresponded to fall for the arctic coast, I suppose.

I was rather surprised when the twenty or so people who had launched the boat all got into it to go on the trip. Of course, we needed some helpers, but all these wouldn't leave much room for wood, especially as pushed by a 1 ½-horse kicker. Another thing-I had got Abraham enthusiastic over the idea of getting our houses jointly supplied with wood toward the winter, since we both lived here. I had made promises about wood to Connie. Several trips like this would solve our fuel problem. But if all these people came along, would not they, too, be entitled to share in the community wood? Well, I guessed that would be all right. I couldn't help it, anyway.

With the whaleboat we headed for the farthest sandspit of the Jones Islands, several miles away. The men-Abraham, old Samuel, Johnny, and I-made the boat safe at the island and picked up a little wood. We then set up Abraham's primus stove to cook dinner. Meanwhile the women, including Mary, Samuel's married daughter, who had a three-months-old baby under her parka, had picked up nearly all the wood which was gathered. The small boys spent their time throwing stones at the phalaropes, which swam about in circles and would fly up and light again.

There were Eskimo footprints all over the sandspit. The drift had been sorted again and again. What was left was mostly old cottonwood trunks; when you sunk an ax into one the water poured out. We picked up little sticks usually no larger than a man's wrist. In a short while some caribou meat from Abraham's ice cellar, cut into chunks, had come to a rolling boil. Abraham's gasoline stove was shut off, we all got a piece of meat on the end of our knives, and once again my teeth ground shut with the familiar crunch of sand. The slab of raw caribou back fat was passed around and we each cut off a slice to eat as one might cut a slice from a cheese.

The sun was low, turning the sea to gold and rose as our whaleboat rocked over the oily swells with sail unfurled and a wind pushing us from behind, toward Beechey Point's buildings that once more seemed to stand in the sea. The musical chortles and chuckles of the Eskimo language about me were already familiar in my ear; the ancient tongue seemed to belong to this land, lending it charm and repose. Johnny steered with that competent nonchalance that only an Eskimo possesses.

This was the only attempt we made that I recall to put in winter's fuel. Other matters immediately came up which prevented further action in this matter. The whaleboat's load was dumped on the beach and we all went to it to get an armful of sticks day by day; the wood rapidly disappeared as used by the entire village.

The day after the wood-getting expedition Abraham climbed up on top of the tall trading post. I shall always remember him there on top of the house; it is one of the most familiar poses in which I can recall Beechey Point Eskimos. They love to get up on some elevation and lookout over the prairie or over the sea; they are always looking for game. Abraham had his binoculars, so I took mine up and joined him on the big peaked roof. From this vantage point Abraham and I looked far out to sea, where the large floes showed plainly out beyond the island reefs.

"Look like good day for ugrug hunt," Abraham said at last. "People around here," he smiled, "they fierce for ugrug skin."

I imagine most of us will soon be familiar with the term ugrug. This word, like igloo, is well on its way to being permanently adopted into the English language to enrich our general vocabulary. We have no English word for this animal-the giant bearded seal of the arctic, which is so important in arctic economy. This giant seal weighs about as much as a medium-sized moose, or as much as 800 pounds; its beard is composed of bristles several inches long and as big around as lollipop sticks at the base where they are attached on his cheeks. Big and glassy are his eyes, protruding foolishly from a small head. It is the largest mammal hunted in Beechey Point waters aside from the polar bear.

The Eskimos are absolutely dependent on ugrug hide for boot soles that are used in spring, summer, and fall walking. This is the only material they have which can stand up to cutting by ice and immersion in water. In some areas we understand the hide of the walrus is similarly used for boot soles, but there is no walrus in this part of the arctic. Common seal is used occasionally on the soles of house boots and it is used on most of the fancy boots which are sold to the tourists who come to Alaska, but common seal is a mere substitute for ugrug and is vastly inferior; it will hardly last for a day's walk.

We simply had to have ugrug soles for the sealskin boots Nanny was already making, but all of the Eskimos replied in turn that they had no ugrug hide which they could spare us, since they needed all they possessed for themselves. They should have had some extra hide saved from last summer's hunting, but of course they did not, and as yet no move was being made to go out and hunt the ugrug this summer. Abraham's remark suggested that maybe here was a way we could get our boot soles now.

Abraham explained to me atop the trading post that the giant seals climb from the ocean up on top of the ice cakes to sleep during the calm days of summer and fall. To hunt them, a crew goes out with a boat into the pack and motors or paddles among the ice cakes and watches. When an ugrug is sighted, the crew cuts the motor and paddles up very close to get a head shot; the ugrug must be killed instantly by a shot in the brain. Everybody in the hunting crew dresses in a snow shirt of white canvas to simulate ice. Every precaution must be taken not to alarm the timid, voluptuous ugrug, or he will dive off the ice cake and get away.

The ugrug mistakes the white whaleboat and its white gowned passengers for a chunk of ice drifting by his polar vista so long as everyone remains motionless. It all seemed easy as it was explained to me.

Passing out beyond the Jones Islands into the real ice pack, our crew of four men in the whaleboat were soon out of sight of land. Today I had my first close sight of the polar ice pack in summer. Here and there before us lay large masses of ice. They ranged from the size of a department store to half a mile across. This was old grounded ice, stuck on the bottom in eight fathoms. Abraham said we could always run behind this ice and anchor to it if a storm came up, for the ice is the small-boatman's friend.

Except for some ridges where a piece of ice had pushed up over another by pressure at some time, the ice pans were normally as flat and level on top as pieces of snow covered prairie. The snows of winter, sticking to the salty ice, had left drifts that had turned at last to ice themselves, while the warm sun of summer had melted shallow ponds all over the surface of the floes. Any of these ponds removed from the dash of the spray will furnish sweet drinking water for hunters and campers. The old whaling ships always used to get their water in this way, by tying up to a fresh floe adrift in the Arctic Ocean to pump water from one of its ponds. Salty sea ice over a year old itself becomes fresh. Here is how this happens: it can remain as a solid only if the temperature remains lower than 26° F. When the temperature rises above this point the sea ice that is salty begins to melt. But fresh water ice can remain frozen at 32° F. Thus, the more salt the ice contains the lower will be its melting point. Ice that remains with a steady temperature of 32 ° or above cannot contain salt or it would melt.

Sea ice retains its saltiness all through the first winter of its formation until the following summer. Then, just as a wire that is suspended over a block of ice with a weight on each end would cut through the block while ice would form behind it, so does the salt sink through the sea ice. After this sea ice has passed through one summer of existence it is always fresh.

These tests were made by taste. Thus, there may be some traces of salt which a chemical analysis could detect, but we are only discussing pure drinking water here. The outer edges of a cake of drifting ice may have to be hacked off where salt spray has dashed, but within lies fresh ice, as every Eskimo of the arctic knows.

It was upon such a large floe, a grounded one, that we landed. Abraham climbed a tall hummock of ice to look around with his glasses while the rest of us walked about. Johnny stayed in the boat. Our crew consisted of Abraham, Johnny, old Samuel, and me. Women never go out on the ugrug hunts. It seems very likely that no woman, either Eskimo or white, has ever killed an ugrug, and of course very few white men have killed one for that matter. Like the walrus and the whale, the ugrug is pretty much the Eskimo's own game. The Eskimos do not take their women out for the sea hunting, which is something apart from land hunting altogether. Connie could probably have violated Eskimo precedent by going along on this hunt, since I possessed the motor which was taking us, but she had no parka. I didn't have a parka either for that matter, but I had to get us some boot soles some way, and so

I went along. Connie had done a lot of hunting with me in the past, but her hunting desires paled enormously in the face of the hardships which winter hunting in this country means and which even few white men care to take for the fun of the game. I took care of the hunting end of it and had a good time after I got my boots and parka.

This was my first walk upon sea ice. Old Samuel kept a weather eye on me, I noted. I soon realized that quite a few of the little ponds on the floes went right straight down into the ocean where the ice had rotted out. Waves had undercut the floes in places so that one had better look sharp. Footing in places was slippery, too.

A common hair seal came up near the boat, popping his head out of the water to look. Seals are very curious. Johnny scraped upon the bottom of the whaleboat and whistled. The seal dove and popped up closer still, its glassy eyes looking. Johnny fired with his rusty .30-30. Down went the seal a clean miss. Again, we piled into the boat and started the quiet little kicker. Slowly we moved off among the big dreamy ice floes. Another swimming seal popped up. I shot it in the head and it sank. I was to learn that a good percentage of seals shot in the brain while they are swimming in the summer time will not float, which is a very great pity. They sink before your eyes and are lost. Two reasons are usually given by our own observers for this: one is that the salinity of the surface water of the ocean in summer is so lessened that it cannot float seals easily, as it normally does during other seasons. (There are always lanes of water out at sea which are opened by tides and currents moving the big ice fields around, even in winter.) The second reason why seals may sink is that in summer they are not nearly so fat with blubber as they are in the wintertime. A seal which weighs around 150 pounds in winter may lose so much blubber that by summer he may weigh but a mere 80 or 90 pounds. The result is that some seals may float if they are shot dead while swimming in open water in summer, but that most seals do not. Certainly, the waste and loss of seals are terrific in ordinary everyday Eskimo life, from sinking and from poor marksmanship. Leffingwell has said that "as a result of poor marksmanship" he has "calculated the natives wound ten seals for each one they secure." Remember Leffingwell lived on this coast for fourteen years.

We estimate loosely that around a thousand seals are taken yearly by the Eskimos on the north coast of Alaska and that they lose around three thousand in the aggregate. Ugrug kills run around thirty, with a loss of eighty by sinking. The wasteful methods of primitive life should be gradually corrected everywhere in the world today, if we are to have a happy, well-fed world.

Abraham, who had been using the glasses, cried: "Ugrug on top of the ice!" He had spotted one!

The words brought a smile to all faces. Donning our white snow shirts (mine being pulled over my own alpaca-lined jacket), we took up our positions in the boat.

I was to be the marksman because the Eskimos had seen me use my telescope sight. Abraham and I kneeled side by side in the bow of the moving whaleboat; I had my rifle and he had a harpoon. Weathered old Samuel steered from the rear, and Johnny paddled. So far, I hadn't seen the ugrug. What did it look like? We rounded a large floe just as the light fog that hung over that area lifted. There, about three hundred yards distant, slept the ugrug, dark against his white ice background. Every minute or less he would raise his head and survey the surrounding seascape. Then his head would drop down and he would snooze about fifty seconds.

The great timid creature was on guard. He had never seen a man, as certainly not one ugrug out of a million can ever have this opportunity, but he was thinking about polar bears which might be sneaking up with the intent of making a meal off him. Although we have all seen polar bears eating fish in the zoo, that is mainly because we have no ugrugs or seals to feed them. The Eskimos say that the polar bear even kills the great two-ton walrus upon occasion. At any rate, every ugrug you see will be watchful and cautious, for the polar bear is the only possible enemy that ugrugs and seals can know. Around and around the polar basin all of them drift together, and there is not a chance in a lifetime that any of these polar ocean animals will come into contact with any kind of man. But the naturalist knows that there are few creatures on this earth which do not have their parasites and their predators, so that nature has taught them all to be wary many eons ago, before man came along. There is no such thing as a natural paradise in the sense of animals being friendly to each other before "cruel man interfered." That is one of the common misconceptions of our nature enthusiasts. Wild animals are not trusting and tame unless some peculiar circumstance accounts for it; the only tame wild animals are in our parks where we have provided artificial protection from their enemies and supplied them with their food.

When the ugrug raised his head, we froze motionless, except for the steady forward glide of the boat. If one of us moved an eyelash during the ugrug's close scrutiny of us, off the ice cake he would have dived in a splash, to disappear beneath the polar sea. To be on the safe side, he lay right on the edge of the ice cake.

Nearer and nearer we drew. "My, that's a big ugrug," whispered Abraham. He resembled a big fuzzy caterpillar to me. He was of a silver-gray color, I saw now, kind of spotted, with a little head revolving on one end and flippers moving like big fans on the rear. When we were a hundred yards distant, his head came up and he gazed at us intently. "Shoot!" whispered Abraham. I steadied the rifle and placed the telescope cross hairs upon that small brain. The report of the rifle was followed by a dull thud as the bullet drove home. The head fell, and the great body lay still.

Not so the crew. They sprang into action as if the shot had released a spring. A dead ugrug sinks like a stone if he manages to slide off the brink into the water; he would be lost unless we got a harpoon into him at once. Ugrugs are never plentiful but are rather rare animals compared to the infinite numbers of the common seals.

But this ugrug lay motionless and safe as we arrived. The bullet had hit it fair in the brain, causing instant death. It was a big female with no young in evidence. About nine feet long, it was covered from end to end with a silvery coarse hair, exactly like a piece of luxurious upholstery. Its eyes were big and glassy; its claws were six inches long and like butcher knives. The giant seal lives on shrimps and crustacea; its exact feeding habits are hard to verify in its natural state because, since ugrugs are taken during their sleep on top of the ice, their stomachs are always empty or nearly so at that time. They go down underwater to do their feeding around midnight each twenty-four hours.

We brought the boat alongside and the four of us had a struggle rolling it into the whaleboat. There it lay like a big cushion.

It was time for us to eat. Johnny started the primus stove atop the floe where we had cast anchor into the ice; he gave some whitefish a few nonchalant scrapes and threw them into the boiling pot. A pan of black coffee was brewed, and we had coffee, fish, and back fat.

We hunted around and saw three seals basking about a hole on the floe. They lay on the ice like miniature ugrugs. Abraham and I crept as close as we dared. I had given him my other identical telescope to keep, which he had mounted on his own rifle. We both fired together. He killed one seal and I killed another. His seal dived and the third seal dived. Abraham was lucky enough to find his floating beside the hole; my seal was dead on the ice.

The day passed, and we hoisted sail and turned home. Connie and all the women met us on the beach. Several happy times they met us like that. We would be lounging on luxurious ugrug upholstery—two for a boatload—when we came home, all during the late summer and fall.

The cutting up of an ugrug is the women's job. They can dismember the largest animal in no time at all because they know exactly where to disjoint it; the toughness of the animal makes no difference. The men rigged a canvas windbreaker for the women to work behind on the beach and then women, children, and pups crowded around the carcass. There was happy chanting, and a flourish of uluruks, the women's curved knives.

First, Connie said, the women removed the hide with the blubber attached. The blubber was two inches thick. There is no fat dispersed within the meat of the animal as is the case with all the land animals we have seen, but the blubber is a uniform casement running all the way around the outside of the body and quite separate from the rest of it. The body of the animal itself within the casement of blubber is dark red or almost black in color and its bones are very small and hard.

Connie presently saw the stomach and intestines of our first ugrug cleaned, chopped up, and transformed into the piece de resistance of a celebration feast in the form of a kind of raw salad or coleslaw served up in a big dishpan and eaten from china plates with forks inside the trading post. We joined the party, partook of a biscuit and tea, tasted a bite of the salad or kayak as it is called, and thought it tasted a good deal like chopped raw cabbage and raw onions mixed. But you may be sure that the very essence of the ugrug resides in its intestines! About fifty pounds of the boiled black ugrug meat and the salad was consumed in the one sitting by the others. Scientists say that rare minerals and vitamins exist in these digestive juices and enzymes of the stomachs of animals which primitives eat and which most of us find we must take in vitamin capsules, if we are to feel at our best. I may be mistaken, but

Beechey Point

I honestly believe that when it comes to diet, the Eskimos at Beechey Point are fed better than any of us in the civilized nations for all our hue and cry about vitamins, calories, and suchlike.

The blood of the ugrug was drained into buckets and cans as the animal was butchered, to be saved for dog feed. The meat of the carcass was then divided into four even piles, representing the four men of the hunting crew who customarily head four different families. The blubber was stripped from the skin and it was likewise divided into four equal portions. The skin itself was left whole to be pegged down to the ground with wooden pegs; it too would be divided into four parts after it was cured. While common seals taken during a hunt belong to the man who gets them in sea hunting, the ugrug is the joint property of the whole crew, who with one man acting as marksman must co-operate to get it. An ugrug is worth $50 altogether. A man can keep what part of his share he likes and sell the rest to the trading post at any time.

When the meat and blubber of the ugrug were cut up there remained not a spot of blood upon the prairie grass beside the sea. The meat and blubber lay in neat clean piles. George told me to pick my pile.

"How come I choose first, George?"

"You shoot the ugrug," he said. "Abraham, he choose second because he own the boat." The all too numerous daughters of poor old Samuel had taken Connie's place in the butchering while she photographed the doings. Samuel's daughters always helped out at anything like that; there were no hunters in the family to help the old widower and his daughters and they were indigent. Everybody was happy now at the prospect of new boot soles.

The Eskimos prize the blubber of the ugrug for an oil in which they like to dip their caribou meat. Connie and I sold all of ours at once for credit at the store towards the caribou hides we needed, in case anybody brought some in.

Hunting seals on the Arctic Ocean

Hunters under the midnight sun

5

Slowly in our mind's eye the cast of Eskimo characters at Beechey Point, acting upon their icy and windy, age-old stage, falls into arrangement.

Abraham and Dora: Dora is handsome, stout, very strong and a great worker, just twenty-one years old. She is a Point Barrow girl and she went to school there for one year; then she worked for "white ladies" for three years as cook and housekeeper in one of the new little U. S. Weather Bureau houses at Barrow. Feeding dogs, presiding at entertainments, with the innumerable boilings of tea and bakings of bread, acting as Abraham's social hostess for the population of an area of several thousands of square miles with Beechey Point as its nucleus, are an important function, never doubt it! I have seen Dora pick up a cake of ice under each arm and carry them into the house from the ice rack for cooking water. Dora is powerful, built just like a wolverine. And as cute as she can be. When we first came to Beechey Point George Woods told us how, after Abraham's older wife (very fat) had died in the influenza epidemic last spring, Abraham had sledded to Barrow and brought Dora back with him on his sled. George and Nanny, who are moral and religious, thought that this was not quite the proper thing. The morals of Eskimos concerning marriage relationships are extremely strict. We are frequently asked about wife trading and free love as soon as the word "Eskimo" is mentioned, but I shall say right now that romantic writers seem to have capitalized on this interest. Since the missionaries came, at least, the Eskimos in these parts adhere as closely in moral matters to the Christian Bible as they can understand it.

Dora is more religious than is skeptical Abraham. She always says grace before meals and carries her Bible with her. She seemed uneasy before us at first. Her glance follows handsome, virile Abraham. Her lip trembled noticeably one day when she introduced Thelma, Abraham's daughter, to us. Thelma must be around twenty, almost Dora's age-a very "white" looking girl, but a deal of a sulker with an unpleasant personality.

Yet forgotten was any unpleasantness in this relationship when Dora, looking out the window from the kitchen one day, forgot the eternal pile of dishes which she must wash, forgot the housewife and became the child, wanting to play outdoors.

Outside the window Dora could see the village women playing achichigok, a game dear to the Eskimo heart. It is a jumping game, played on a board balanced teeter-totter over a mud hummock. Two girls take their places standing on opposite ends of the board until the board is in balance; then, slowly beginning to rock, they gain momentum. As the board comes down on the ground on one end, the player at the opposite end is catapulted into the air. Higher and higher the players jump each time, sometimes kicking their feet in midair like a dancer. The object seems to be to throw the other player off. Girls and women have always excelled in the Eskimo jumping games. All summer long they play achichigok. As the twilight of the late summer midnight hours begins to fall beside the polar sea, they are all out playing and screaming with delight.

Dora stood it just as long as she could, watching out the window; then she too had to join in. The next we saw, she and Thelma were rolling on the ground together like playful puppies, in hysterics of laughter.

It is give and take with Abraham and Dora, those two, as back and forth they wisecrack in Eskimo, sometimes surprising you in the middle of it by breaking out in an English "Okiedoke." Abraham is considered a very good catch because of his being the trader with a very good living to offer, but Dora is spunky, and she is his match. Abraham, the much sought after, and spunky little Dora have been much criticized and yet are at the same time rather wistfully looked at by the others for their glamorous position. They represented at this time the Country Club set of Beechey Point, you might say.

Beechey Point

Following the two stars comes a long cast of supporting players whom we were coming to know. Next might be Nanny, our "Eskimo mother."

Nanny is one of those awfully good women of the earth. No better woman ever breathed. Connie had had a stream of callers at the house while I was engaged in the wood-hauling and ugrug-hunting projects. The women and children would slip shyly in without knocking-for how can people who have never had doors know the symbol of the closed door or know what knocking means? Connie would offer them a chair. But they were uncomfortable on chairs. Soon Connie learned to let them sit on the floor along the wall, and she would put their food on the floor and sit down to join them in their "tea party," and so would try to keep the floor very clean.

Nanny as our seamstress was naturally one of the first and continued to be the most frequent of these visitors, all of whom were accompanied, of course, by their numerous small children. Presently came Ada, a poor widow. Ada brought with her two lovely round rosy daughters, Jennie and Maria, and her youngest, Mary, age four, who was still nursing between bites of meat. Ada herself is as withered as a fall weed and has a face like a sheep's. Her husband died in the epidemic last winter, leaving her with a family of five. They come from the eastward, but she was unable to tell us more.

Ada was supported in her visit by Virginia, wife of nonchalant Johnny, the ugrug hunter. Virginia is not blessed with beauty and we classified her soon as the poor-relation type, inasmuch as she is not shy, has an immensely large mouth, and is always ready to put into it whatever is handed out. Virginia's children are the raggedest and most ill-kept of urchins and Virginia's dress remains from year to year in a state of chronic filth. Her oldest child, little Dora, is a doll; Donald, the younger, is the typical "problem child" who should have been called Junior. He is always getting into things, where the other little Eskimo children are remarkably well behaved.

On the floor sat Connie with the women, before whom were served the refreshments of the day: tea, some small butter and peanut butter sandwiches, and a large platter of cold sliced roast caribou meat which Ada pronounced "very fine." As they finished eating, Ada and Virginia became interested in the dirt and sand on the floor, which had come in with them on their mukluks, and they began to play with it, shaping it into little piles with their fingers, because they were embarrassed about having made dirt in the clean house. When Donald wet the floor the poor widow Ada shyly began mopping up the dirty floor with a clean diaper which she had brought with her, until Connie caused her to desist in this unnecessary solicitude.

Ada had a motive in calling. Her daughter Jennie had brought with her some fancy house slippers trimmed with red-dyed sealskin and white fox fur, which she wanted to sell. The slippers again were too small for Connie. Furthermore, they did not have ugrug soles, but at Connie's suggestion Jennie indicated that she could make some more just like them in her size. The little girl was justly proud of her sewing, and besides the fact that Nanny had been so busy sewing for her own family that she had hardly yet got to us was the fact that the poor fatherless family seemed sadly to need the money. Why not have this extra family, Ada and her daughters, sew for us too, and give them the work, reasoned Connie.

Often, we had observed Ada and her daughters getting a handout in the Woodses' large tent, and it seemed to Connie justly fitting that they should make this effort towards self-support and self-respect. Yet while sorely tempted to conclude this business right away, Connie only went so far as to allow Jennie to draw the size of her foot on a piece of paper and then told the family that she must talk it over with me. We had agreed always to use the method of having one-person deal with the Eskimos to avoid any confusion as to what was meant.

I agreed subsequently that it would be nice to have the little girl do the work. I had to go to Nanny's tent, and I spent three hours there explaining. There is no use trying to hide anything in such a community. I had been a small-town boy myself. All deals are known and discussed by everyone; Ada was Nanny's best woman friend. I thought I had better explain Connie's little deal directly to George in English so there could be no misunderstanding among the women, because we had meant to keep our sewing in one family from the first. The lesson herein related cannot be overestimated in its importance in dealing with Eskimos, and perhaps with other people as well.

Nanny arrived at our house one morning, having completed a pair of sealskin water boots for me. She made these in two days once she got started. The new boots were generously praised and of course we were very glad to have them. I went off ugrug hunting with the fellows, while

Beechey Point

Nanny lingered over tea and sweet bread with Connie before returning to her own house. Up till now we had all been the best of friends and Connie had taken a great liking to this capable motherly woman with her wise twinkling eyes. Little did Connie know the trouble brewing, but just as Nanny was about to leave, Connie gave to her Jennie's small slippers which had been left at the house as samples and asked Nanny if she would return them to Jennie. Since Ada and her girls practically lived with Nanny, and possessed only a small sleeping tent of their own, this had seemed a natural thing to do. At once our good Nanny flared. She was jealous! She was jealous that any work might be given, no matter how small, to the other family! Her pride was touched. "Does my sewing not please?"

Connie tried to explain that she had thought Nanny was too busy to make slippers for her, and how Jennie was just a little girl. Nanny's opinion of this differed. Jennie, sixteen, was a grown woman. Connie tried to search for words which the Eskimo woman knew, and felt herself getting more and more involved in the emotionalism of a dangerous subject the longer it was dwelt upon. Nanny immediately suggested, "My girl, Martha, she do fine sewing." Martha is fourteen, and her fancywork we already knew and appreciated, but no inducement thus far had succeeded in getting any of her work done for us. The main point, too, to Connie, had been to help the other family whom Nanny and George Woods had to support as paupers anyway. Yet Nanny could not see this. Nanny was like many of us who enjoy helping our neighbor-we do not like to see our neighbor become independent of us to the point where he no longer needs our support.

Of course, if Nanny's sense of importance was hurt, we might just up and lose our seamstress upon whom we were utterly dependent, in a flash-just like that! People, but especially Eskimos, work for you in this Alaska land only if they like you, and if they don't like you, no money can buy them. A fine way to be, too, Connie had to admit to herself, tongue in cheek. Suddenly frantic at our own personal danger of being without a seamstress and fearful of having ruined everything that I had accomplished with my own diplomatic relations with the Eskimos, Connie retracted her most cherished ideals: she simply thrust the pitiful little slippers at Nanny and said, "Tell Jennie no, no! No good!"

Nanny's face lighted in a smile of triumph and gone were the sulks.

The good woman left, extracting a promise from Connie to come to visit her at her tent this afternoon about the sewing. How she did this, with her small command of English and Connie's large command of it, remains insoluble. Eskimos are great traders and bargainers from away back.

When Connie got to Nanny's tent that afternoon, she was grateful to be received. She made the arrangement for Nanny's daughter Martha to make her house boots at once. George, sitting there, explained that his wife was not so busy now because "she waits for hides," and "has the time now to make the little things."

Connie had to step over to Ada's tent next door to say hello, as she was afraid the family, having her foot size, might have even started the deadly slippers. Jennie was not at home. Home only was Ada of the sheep like face, crouched miserably upon the floor in her rags, in a hovel no larger than a dog-house for one dog. Receiving the pretty slippers back, Ada smiled her wan smile. It was an ample revenge for the hurt pride of Nanny; Connie's heart filled with pity for the poor wretch whom she had been forbidden to assist on peril of herself being cold in the winter.

"Let the Eskimos take care of their own charity problems," I was forced to tell Connie. "They have taken care of themselves for a long time before now, we have little power here, and that only to observe."

For such reasons were Connie and I unable to engage other seamstresses at Beechey Point, when our clothing seemed slow in materializing.

The next character in our cast is Abraham's daughter Thelma. She looks so much like a white girl at times that it is strange to see her among all the other Eskimo women. Abraham tells us Thelma wants to go Outside to live-meaning to the United States. He treats her with good-humored tolerance, but hardly with full approval, and we wondered for a long time if she might not be a little queer, for she would never smile or speak when spoken to. How much English she understands we still do not know for sure, but quite a good deal, apparently. Often, she looks as though she had been crying. Early in the morning we can see her from our window walking along the beach alone, and we have longed to help her if we only knew how, but she rebuffs us coldly. She plays the great lady around Beechey Point and is probably regarded as a snob. But the great lady is far from happy. I should say that Dora is her only real friend. How often Dora would serve us black coffee, bread made with hops, hamburger patties of ground caribou, and fish fried white man style, and Thelma would not even appear at the table but would eat alone. Abraham seems to eat a great many fried foods and he asserts, for instance, that boiled meat, Eskimo style, gives him indigestion. Both he and Thelma have digestive disturbances. For this we have no explanation except that obviously poor Abraham and Thelma are trying to get away from those superficial attributes of Eskimo life which they believe to be the important differences between their station and the station of white people. Abraham wants to get Thelma married to some young man of the community-he doesn't care who-but there doesn't appear to be a very good chance of that, since she is so disagreeable.

Johnny and Virginia, town loafers, are a pair for you. Every town in America has their counterpart. In civilization we goad such people in our efforts to make all people alike and up to standard, until the poor devils eventually lose their minds and must be put into an institution, whereupon we care for them anyway in the end. The Eskimos are more tolerant of each other than we. They never criticize anyone too seriously and never appear to notice if he works or not, and the amount of work each individual does varies a good deal, according to his temperament and circumstances. All do not do an equal share of work in an Eskimo community, but each does what he can, and somehow the work gets done. Johnny here gets along winter after winter without a parka to his back. Last year he didn't catch so much as a single fox. Someday he may find himself unexpectedly in the position of a party Abraham told us about five hunters who were drifted out to sea on an ice floe and couldn't get back to shore for several days. An offshore gale came up and they were separated from shelter in the breaking floes and had no fuel. Of the five, two men got back alive and the other three were frozen to death because their parkas were not sufficient to stand the test of storm and gale. Yet Johnny will never worry about having this happen to him until it happens. So far, he has got by in the kind of clothing which the average town bum might wear around a city park and that's all he has had all winter. Abraham, who supports half the people who live on this coast out of his own resources, helps the family by giving Johnny and homely Virginia a handout in the nick of time.

Mr. Lynd and his blind wife Mart walked six miles to Beechey Point from their inland home, Mart carrying her youngest, Donald, on her back and taking Lucy by the hand. She and the children came to visit our house, guided by Hazel. Hazel is one of the village orphans. She is eleven years old, dressed completely in skins. She wears what is cast off and is passed around from family to family along the coast. The Lynds have had her of late. I think Hazel has the most beautiful smile and the biggest, happiest rose-red cheeks I have ever seen in my life on any human being. The little waif is a great worker, in vigorous animal health, and she is a favorite with all. She is at the age where she seemingly has no sex, but carries wood with the boys or hunts caribou with them on the flowering summer prairies and whatever. I don't believe that anybody here realizes that Hazel is going to be a very beautiful woman someday. Hazel has nothing in the world, no people, no dowry. Old Lynd and his blind wife can, of all the Eskimos, probably least afford to feed another mouth. Kind old Lynd. And so Hazel came leading Lynd's blind wife Mart and the younger children into our house, and they sat on the floor, bringing much sand on their mukluks.

They ate everything that was offered, which was a good deal that day, because Connie was feeling in an expansive mood. She would always try to treat everybody a little special who came from out of town. Nanny's expression was surprised when the blind woman, who has but small social position, what with her aged husband and no older boys for hunters in the family, was entreated to stay longer. Blind Mart could speak some English and she was the first among the Eskimos to call Connie by her first name, and it came to her lips with such naturalness that Connie loved the blind woman from the first. Connie said she enjoyed seeing Nanny's mouth fly open for, from her close associations with the white people as well as by her almost daily entertainments in the "big house" of Abraham, Nanny had come to swell almost perceptibly with that sense of well-being which is so common among some of our own society matrons.

Andrew the preacher was one of the biggest cataclysms to hit Beechey Point, and you may be sure that Nanny was one of the first to get upon the inside track with this celebrity. Everybody knows that Andrew and his wife Susie (Presbyterian, not ordained) are the highest ranking of hoi polloi over at Barter Island to the eastward. An experience for the album of memory was the reflection of the native minister's family launch anchored off Beechey Point the night he came to us, with the sun bursting through the clouds in a strange golden glory, just as it was about to set below the horizon at approximately eleven o'clock. Connie was just about to go to bed, when she stepped out of the house for a breath of air. The temperature was forty-four degrees by our wall thermometer. The Arctic Ocean was like a blue mirror. As she looked out over the silent expanse and the mirrored anchored launch from Beechey Point there were ice cakes on the horizon and over them a kind of rainbow in pink, green, and violet about twenty degrees to each side of the sun. It was a parhelion, or parhelia-plural, we know now. This is a mock sun or bright light seen near the sun, caused by crystals in the air. The parhelia or sundogs are a peculiarity of the Arctic Ocean and it is a rare sight to see a good one.

Into Connie's vision across the fish nets bobbing before our door there came then a man and a boy, probably his son, rowing in a boat. We don't know now who they were and what does it matter? They were singing. First one would chant in a high tenor, then the other would take up the thread of the song, to the accompaniment of lusty swinging oars. It was a wild song, in minor, some Eskimo story or legend of olden days sung out to the Arctic Ocean and the shimmering mysterious sundogs as they rowed.

It was the next day that Andrew the preacher commenced to hold regular services in the Eskimo language for the people who would gather in the big house or in the tent of George and Nanny Woods, where he had taken up residence. Andrew got $800 a year from a mission society in the United States for helping to spread the faith. You had to say that as soon as you went into a room with him, among forty-two people present, you would know at once that he was the minister. There must be something that makes ministers all alike in any race or clime: the beatific smile, the hearty handclasp, fairly call you to the fold. He was the only person sitting up off the floor upon a chair, and that's good psychology in itself. Connie declined the chair he offered her in good fellowship and sat down upon the flooring with the others, taking her place by the side of the widow Ada.

Andrew is a born leader of people and a born politician. He is unusually tall for what we had expected an Eskimo to be-but again we are getting used to this. He is around six feet two and has a large nose. He has a stentorian speaking and singing voice. I can best describe his importance to these people by saying that just before services Connie had a group of boys at the house for tea and cakes-Connie was well liked by the little boys, who carried her wood for her and two of the Barter Island visitors were among these, when suddenly one of them looked out the window and the visitors rose as one. "There he comes!" said one in English, and they were off.

Andrew speaks the most intelligible English of anyone yet. He was the first Eskimo who actually asked us questions about ourselves, as to what we thought of Beechey Point, and so forth, and the first to lead the conversation himself. He has been much with missionaries and was once offered the opportunity to go on tour in the United States for a year to display himself as an Eskimo convert, with all expenses paid. He considered it a long time, but turned down the chance because he said he was fearful that the climate of the south would be too hot for him and he was worried that his health might break down; along with this was the point that he felt he would not be able to get along on the kind of foods he would have to eat in civilization, as he had great trust in the meat upon which he had always lived. We gave Andrew our last quarter of a pound of tea and he said gratefully, "Thank you, thank you. My seven sons and the families at Barter Island, we will like it much. I am careful with my tea. Each time in the water that boils, just one teaspoon."

"Yes," I thought of Barter Island, "I expect they boil the grounds three times over and then chew them." It looked as if we wouldn't any of us be getting any grub from Barrow this year again, so what good did money do you if you had it? I had an idea that Andrew's sermons, which were taken altogether from the Old Testament, had been heard many times at Beechey Point. When he would leave finally to go back home, I suspected that there would be a sigh of relaxation, much as his next visit would be looked forward to.

And now we jump back to the Woods family to find the little crippled child, George and Nanny's daughter Martha, age fourteen! She had struck us oddly by her large limpid eyes and pale, perfect ivory complexion framed by the dark wolverine fur of her hood, and by her generally fragile appearance, from the time we first saw her crouched with her fancy sewing in the back of the Woods tent. If seen with her parka off, in only a house dress, that child is just a shadow. We thought her beautiful, according to Western ideas, but wondered instantly if she might not have tuberculosis. Later we came to believe not, but we saw that she does have a peculiar dragging walk. Martha lost both her older brother, the one just younger than Apiak, and a sister at Foggy Islands in the epidemic of influenza. Abraham lost his own wife from influenza, Ada lost her husband from it, and one of Matthew's daughters up the Colville was left widowed with five children when her husband, who had brought the "cold" on a return trip from Barrow, died beside his sled on the trail where he was found a week later when some of his dogs came home. Gentle old Samuel lost his wife and two of his grown daughters at the same time. Old Samuel, for an Eskimo, has the saddest face I have ever seen; you see he loved his wife very much. One fifth of the Beechey Point population, or that is the population drained from an area of several thousand square miles, had succumbed to this terrible germ just three months before we came.

The peculiar point of the whole thing was that Barrow, the place to which one would naturally look for succor, had suffered much worse than the scattered people. Our epidemics out Beechey Point way always come from Barrow. Our people got the sickness by taking the furs to Barrow in the spring and they brought the illness back with them.

Eskimos and Indians do not thrive in crowded conditions. Under the conditions of the greatest civilization or settlement they have proved themselves to be especially susceptible to disease because their systems have no natural immunization to European imported bacteria. The village at Point Barrow is under quarantine for a good portion of each year due to one germ or another that gets started among the population. This is the usual thing there and has been going on for at least the last fifty years. Poverty, indolence, moral lassitude, and disease thrive more abundantly than ever, before the very doors of the school, church, trader, and government hospital which have attracted large numbers of the Eskimos to settle down and live there. We had already heard the story of Barrow's last winter epidemic from the Seabees at Umiat, some of whom had spent time at Barrow and were quite explosive in their opinions about it. They had a great deal of blame to lay upon the government agencies which have set themselves up there to be responsible for these dying Eskimos, yet which are not keeping the Eskimos from dying. The navy fellows had seen Eskimos lying on the cold floors of their filthy unheated shacks, piled so thick you couldn't step over the bodies, in different stages of dying and dead. The beautiful government hospital erected to care for them could not contain them all. There was no fuel at Barrow to heat the hospital. Not enough fuel oil had come on the single ship North Star the year before. Then why wasn't fuel supplied by airplane or the Eskimo patients flown to other Territorial hospitals? the Navy asked. Well, that's easy to ask but a big order for civilian agencies to fill. Alaskans know the answers to some of these questions better than the Outsider. This condition has been going on for a long time, and it is just that Alaska is yet an undeveloped country which needs help in these things.

But the Navy at Point Barrow in the year 1945-1946 was profoundly shocked by the civilian conditions that it saw there. White civilians weren't affected; they were all taken care of by their own stocks of commissary goods and fuel had been arranged for them by the various government departments which they represented, with considerable foresight. It was the native civilian conditions that were a shock. The Navy issued emergency fuel to run the hospital for the sick Eskimos and went into the Eskimo tents and houses and carried the sick Eskimos bodily into their own hospital units, where they were bathed and clothed and many were nursed back to life with the latest techniques.

Our little friend Martha was affected by these general conditions in an interesting way. Connie wanted to make sure the child rode in on the boat, if it came to Beechey Point this summer, to go to the hospital. Martha is an orthopedic case. Something had gone out of joint in her back, possibly owing to some unrealized fall or strain in early adolescence; she was not aware of the accident when it occurred, but gradually she had grown into a cripple without any correction for this condition. At the free government hospital for the Eskimos at Barrow Martha could be given expert care by the doctor and correction if she and her people could be brought to see the wisdom of it.

But George and Nanny, grieved as they are about the strange affliction of their beloved oldest daughter, accept the affliction with fatalism, bowing to "the inevitable," and they will not send Martha to the hospital. In a way, you could not but wonder if there could indeed be some merit in their point of view, when you know better the situation at Barrow. They love Martha, she is almost all they have now of their family, and she is so frail anyway. They do not dare to send her to Barrow, knowing that so many people die there!

Ice was forming every night on the inland ponds of the prairie;

Beechey Point

summer was almost gone. No supply boat had come from Barrow, despite the fact that it was an open season and a boat could have got through weeks ago. Our people growled audibly to us about the management of their own store. The Barrow Native Store runs its business on a shoestring, so that the corporation is generally out of goods long before the North Star has come in each year from the Pacific Ocean.

"Maybe we could go to Point Barrow in the whaleboat," I finally said to worried Abraham, who had used all of his powers of subtlety upon me for some time. "I guess we could get there with my kicker," I said. An idea had come into my mind, which turned out to be completely erroneous, that possibly an effort was being made to "starve out" our valiant group of individualists at Beechey Point by cutting off their supplies intentionally, to drive them to live with the more settled Eskimos at the Point Barrow village beside school and church. If this was true, I was ready to investigate it, for I like individualists. It was not true, but it added to the lure of seeing famous Point Barrow, Uncle Sam's farthest north point of land, which I had heard of all my life since I was a little kid at school but had never expected to get to see.

"Yes, maybe we better go over to Barrow ourself," Abraham agreed congenially, "and see what in hell is matter with them they not sent us food for two years. No grub around here, no shells, no nothing. People are out of everything and these women get mad at me. I do not know what to say to them."

And so, it was that Connie and I found ourselves preparing to start for legendary Point Barrow, 240 miles away, with the old whaleboat and our kicker to get food for the Beechey Point Eskimos. There were six of us who went. Abraham and Dora, spunky and jolly as usual, and having a dickens of a good time out of it; Abraham's daughter Thelma the deal of a sulker, wearing much lipstick; saddened, gentle old Samuel, carrying his Bible with him (having been much influenced of late by the visit of the minister), and Connie and I. We didn't have quite enough gasoline left in our supplies to get us there, but we did have a big sail and the dependable east wind behind us would help to blow us along. There would be plenty of white man's grub for us all when we got there.

Cutting up the ugrug is women's work

Little Eskimo girl

We arrive in Barrow, fall 1945

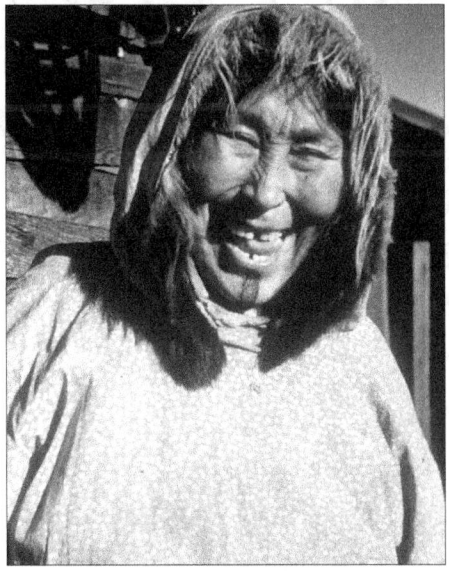

Old woman at Point Barrow

Unloading back at Beechey Point

Eskimo elders

Cutting ice to store for summer use

Abraham brings in a load of driftwood

Abraham tells the dogs, "Go lie down"

Bud fills cans with water

6

We were supposed to leave for Point Barrow on a Monday. Next, we would leave late Monday night or early Tuesday morning. Our sleep was uneasy as we waited in our clothes to be called at any moment from our Beechey Point home. All day Tuesday passed, and we sat waiting. At nine Tuesday evening I lay down on the bed in my clothes-our bed this year was a door laid over packing boxes-to get a wink while waiting for Abraham to be ready. By eleven that night, Connie made me go over to Abraham's house, dignity or no dignity, and find out what was wrong. I found him there struggling heroically with his bookkeeping.

By noon Wednesday a glance out of our window toward the trading post told us that Abraham's house was sound in slumber, sleeping, no doubt, the sleep of the exhausted. No smoke was coming from the chimney. An Eskimo community moves at its own pace and you can't hurry it.

About then a storm came on which blew for the next three days. On August 31 we actually embarked. "This would be good practice grounds for a chronic worrier," Connie mentioned. "He would either be completely cured for the rest of his life after a year with the Eskimos or he would die of the cure. Do you realize, my dear, what I'm thinking? I'm thinking that we are just likely to get frozen in at Point Barrow or halfway between, and not be able to get back at all, because this crazy ocean is about to freeze."

Yes, the more sheltered bays along the shore were freezing every night now with young ice which would soon be too thick for the whaleboat to buck. "Oh, we'll come back by dog team after the freeze-up if we get stuck at Barrow," I told her. "That's the way Abraham got back after last summer and that's why the Beechey Point cargo boat is at Barrow now. It got frozen in there last fall."

Connie and I now at last had the Eskimo type of sealskin summer boots with ugrug soles. We had an excellent pair of white wolf mittens between us bought from Abraham, and I had his left-over reindeer-skin parka, for my own. Apiak had not been too successful in the hunt this summer for caribou, and after having supplied his own family first was even now out hunting for the hides which were supposed to make our winter parkas. Thelma had been obliged to lend Connie one of her own, a new fawnskin parka, for the trip. To Thelma a trip to Point Barrow meant an adventure in high society and one could almost feel her disappointment about not being able to wear her new fawnskin parka.

Then just before we left for Barrow, I discovered that our motor was broken. Some Eskimo couldn't resist playing with it when I wasn't around, and he twisted the needle valve into the motor as hard as he could and broke it off inside. Now it must have taken some brains to do that! I don't know how many hours I worked to get in there with a small instrument and actually fix the thing. As Abraham had told us that the Beechey Point people never have enough meat to eat, our urgency to reach Barrow was further increased by the thought that if for some reason it was a bad season and the usual fish and game were not obtainable, there was indeed a possibility of actual starvation for the group out here, especially if we couldn't get them ammunition.

The gray waves rolled roughly under the whaleboat as we started out on our cold 240-mile ocean journey. We had made a tent over the top for shelter and we lay upon bags and sacks within, while one of us navigated from the rear where the little motor was installed. There were going to be two big bays to cross on the way. Harrison Bay is about ninety miles across and it can get plenty rough. Smith Bay is almost as bad. Abraham hoped the ice pack would be in Harrison Bay so as to make the water calmer and protect us from the open ocean. If it got too rough, we could always tie up behind the ice. It was not thinkable to go into these bays and around by the shore line because they are too shallow; the shallows can be extremely dangerous in a high wind, as any sailor knows. The shallow bays are the main hazard which would caution me to advise anyone in a small boat not to try a trip from Beechey Point to Barrow along the north Alaska coast. Nobody goes into these bays. The Eskimos know only the route straight across the ocean and do not know the shore line in detail. In winter they cross the bays by sled.

We landed upon Thetis Island, which is directly opposite the mouth of the Colville River, far out of sight of land, in a gray and stormy sea. As it was too rough to start across Harrison Bay, we set up our little wood stove inside our tent pitched on the sand, cooked meat, and slept. Connie had brought some baked stuff in a sack and Abraham had with him the last twenty-five-pound sack of flour possessed by Beechey Point. Two five-gallon gas cans used for containers of whitefish supplied the rest of the provisions for our journey. Next day the wind continued and much black in the sky-what we call "water sky"-showed us that there was but little ice in Harrison Bay beyond our horizon ahead. Thetis Island, a bleak strip of land not four feet high, as a new experience to Connie and me because it was our first arctic island. It was covered with scattered patches of light snow and looked completely unreal; upended ice cakes, as large as California bungalows, stood nearby, stranded and grounded on the side of the beach. They were blue, white, and green.

The ice pack presses all about here at all times of the year, but we trusted that the Eskimos calmly camping here knew what they were doing. They seemed perfectly at home. Sleet was sheeting the tent when delighted screams of "Navy! Navy!" came from Dora who was washing fish along the water's edge. Out of the foggy gray sea there hove two launches! The excitement and joy of our crowd at bumping into these friends at barren Thetis Island knew no bounds. "We jumped up and down with glee on the beach and shouted our lungs out. I looked at Connie and she looked back at me. We knew our troubles were over. These boats were forty feet long, with a width amidships of eleven feet. One had in fact formerly belonged to the Navy, but they were Native Store Boats now; they were not manned by the "Navy" as we had at first thought in our excitement, but they were manned by an all-Eskimo crew who were well-known friends and relatives of our Beechey Point Eskimos. The cargo boats, each powered with a twenty-horsepower gasoline engine, and decked over with a heavy framework covered by canvas, had been looking for us, in fact. They had already been to Beechey Point and dumped a load of oatmeal and flour on the beach and were at this time returning to Barrow for a second trip for rations. Their navigators had been informed of our departure towards Barrow in the whaleboat, and they knew that we would be camped at this familiar spot on Thetis Island. Therefore, they came right here for us. It was really as simple as all that!

Gone instantly were the grudges and queries of our Eskimos, in their good nature. Forgotten already was the letter Abraham carried in his pocket to the store manager at Barrow, asking, "Why you not do your job?" Fur-hooded Eskimo faces hung out of every side of the dumpy cargo boats with big smiles from everybody there on Thetis Island in the foggy sea.

Crawling inside the dark interior of one of these boats, we saw first what appeared to be crowds of people, including, of course, the inevitable women and children who travel with the Eskimos wherever they go, many of whom had come along for the ride. We were given bread and coffee with sugar and milk. Cooking was done on board by a primus stove which gave out but little warmth, and the atmosphere inside the boat was as chill and damp from the sea as our own whaleboat had been. But we all lived in our parkas and so were quite comfortable. The Eskimos treated us as guests. Within the hour, willing hands had struck our camp and we were all off to Barrow in the largest make of boat which plies the Arctic Ocean today-forty feet long, which seemed large then, but somehow such a boat looks small when I see it in a picture now.

From Thursday noon until Saturday midnight we traveled.

The trip was a rough one, cold, foggy, and damp. The worst of it was the gasoline fumes from the ill-treated and leaky inboard motor which made the air inside these boats perfectly blue. Connie and all the girls and women lay in a row on some piles of skins with a can at their heads as the boat commenced to roll. The navigator, when he went out side at the stern to take his turn, had a chance to come to, but of course he was glad to come in again and take his place among the rows of bodies after a few hours of dodging ice cakes with the sleet in his face; his parka would be dripping icicles. At long intervals our boat would touch shore to allow us all to get out, if it were possible to make the leap from the bow without landing in the shallows. People merely moved off a few steps and turned their backs or the women huddled underneath their parkas with the children to fulfill the wants of nature. In this country there is no privacy to be found behind hills or bushes. There is not even a log. It is so flat and barren that you could see a billiard ball for eight miles in every direction were there a billiard ball to see. Connie said the main thing that turned her stomach inside out on the trip was to lie inside the rolling boat as we traveled and watch the small children jump on and off the flywheel of the engine while their phlegmatic parents looked on. Why native children don't lose all their hands and legs before they grow up seems a miracle; if accidents occur, as they do rarely, they are generally accepted with resignation.

Eskimo children are generally shy around strangers; they are more modest and better-mannered than white children. They play heartily but a good deal more quietly on the whole because their games do not deal with modern warfare or tommy guns and the noise of the atomic age but deal with such situations as stalking imaginary game or imitating the dignified lives their parents lead. Eskimo voices are soft and modulated, and the child imitates. It appears easier, at that, to raise ten Eskimo children under primitive conditions than one white child under our conditions of today if we can judge by the ease with which these people do it.

At the beginning of each day as we traveled Dora came over from Abraham, who was one of the pilots on the other boat, and cooked breakfast for Connie and me-at least for me. I changed boats now and then, and so the time passed. If you wanted to change boats, you signaled the other craft and it pulled alongside. You then jumped to the other boat, taking care not to jump into the Arctic Ocean. Connie stayed where she was.

It was midnight when we cast anchor off Point Barrow. Because the days had shortened the night was dark now. The airplane beacon making its periodic rounds flashed a friendly welcome across the arctic sky, its moving beams speaking of the white man's civilization with all that means to the lonely traveler. We slept on board. It was about nine the next morning when we were able to put in.

First came the new naval base. It lay out on the long sand spit toward the point. I am sure the reader has noticed my references to Barrow and then to Point Barrow. The village of Barrow is not really on the point at all. The true Point Barrow runs roughly eight or ten miles on north. Several pilots, including Wiley Post, who cracked up with Will Rogers near here, have had difficulty in finding the village of Barrow because they expected the town to be upon the point while in reality it is several miles from it.

Along the point now lay piles of gasoline drums racked up; new hangars were in the process of being built and caterpillars scuttled, while trucks, weasels, and cranes stood about. Down the long line of beach presently appeared a group of soldiers standing around the flames of an open bonfire built of scrap lumber. Now that's a sight all of us will always remember who have known modern-day Alaska with its construction camps and bases. Those fellows always look so cold! Near the men standing beside the fire, Eskimo women and children could be seen searching the ocean front for driftwood or whatever they could find. At Point Barrow, as everywhere else in the world, natives scavenge the United States Army and Navy dumps. One little girl rowed a boat through the gray waves. The Eskimos had been practically subsisting off the navy garbage piles here for many months; they did little trapping for foxes, but in response to the demand for carved ivory trinkets of the walrus tusks spent their time in the souvenir business, or just loafing, taking in the show. As a result, some of them had money in their pockets and there was a certain boom in the trade at Barrow, with the Eskimos taking full advantage of the opportunity to increase their prices for souvenirs and handiwork; but their money was almost worthless because they were unable to buy the things for mere existence at the isolated outpost. There is a chronic shortage of even matches. The people have no caribou skins for parkas and some have bought imported cotton or woolen blankets at fabulous prices from independent white traders or subsidized civilians, out of which "blanket parkas" are made. The fault of not being able to get goods does not lie with the Native Store alone-nobody can get enough because of the physical obstacles involved in freighting goods into this ocean. Almost no food of any sort can be bought in the village from the Native Store or other traders at this time of year. All of their stocks are depleted. The several hundred Eskimos therefore were subsisting from day to day on a little seal meat secured by a few hunters who possessed gasoline for their boats, meat which sold on the market at that time at five cents a pound, and by scavenging from the navy dump along the waterfront waiting for the ship North Star to come. This sight is repeated year by year, depending on Barrow's occupation by various forces and expeditions.

There is always a shortage of meat at Point Barrow, for when you take a people who have always made their living by hunting and settle them down in one community to live, it is obvious that there will be a problem in getting enough meat locally to feed such a number. The meat shortage was acute now, as no whales had been killed this summer, and it takes from four to six whales to support the six hundred or so natives and their dogs yearly at Barrow in the style to which they have been accustomed.

As for fuel, you can walk a hundred miles out of Point Barrow in either direction along the beach and not find a stick of wood the size of a match. Every stick has been picked up long before this time.

Originally when the Eskimos burned seal oil and whale oil in stone lamps within their tiny, well-insulated igloos made of skins and snow blocks, wood was not the valuable article to them that it is now. It never occurred to the Eskimos to burn wood! Wood was used only for implements and making things. It was the white man who taught them to burn wood in stoves, and today they are as helpless without it as any of us would be in their position. Discarded gasoline packing boxes which can be picked up around the naval base or which come with the traders' orders of gasoline on the North Star sell for stove wood at Barrow for fifty cents each. The white residents there are not affected by this; of course, they have their fuel oil provided for them and their houses are heated by modern heating plants the year around.

The shortage of meat and fuel at Barrow is the main reason why Beechey Point people and Barter Island people have refused, wisely perhaps, to go there to live and be "civilized." They would all like to have their children a tend school, and they all adore church services, but they retain their independence, even to running out of the last rifle shell and the last sack of flour, before they will conform to the hardship of trying to live at Barrow. Thus, they remain today's most "primitive" and most prospering native people left now under the American flag.

Most of our people in the eastern ocean have relatives living at Barrow. Of course, Barrow was originally a large Eskimo village anyway, dating back into antiquity long before the white man came, because it is an ideal hunting site for the sea animals on which the village has always principally lived. There is no sensible reason why

Point Barrow people should ever be hungry today any more than they were formerly because the resources of the mighty Arctic Ocean are endless if the people will work. Barrow is no fishing site, and there are not the runs of whitefish which we know along the coast eastward, but the currents around this most hostile appearing of all windy points of the earth are really friendly to the Eskimos because they keep the water pretty well open all year around. Here, since long ago, have always lived a large number of Eskimos in the very teeth of the gale, thriving as only they knew how. Here pass the walrus, following their ancient migration routes, veering off toward Siberia's shores, carried by the warmer currents of the Bering Sea. Here hard by come the great black whales. The whales which come north each summer pass close to land in the deep water off Point Barrow and then, like the walrus, sheer off the continent, so that it is only a rare straggler of even the beluga or small white whale which is seen near shore around Beechey Point. The extreme shallowness of the sea for many miles out makes whaling there impracticable.

Besides the whales and the seals and the walrus to feed the population of Barrow, the very spot upon which the naval base now stands was and still is the point over which the countless millions of eider ducks fly their regular sky trails each spring. Many an Eskimo with a shotgun would stand there and shoot three hundred eiders in a day, as the migrating birds crossed the point, and the sea and the sky were black with calling wild fowl.

There is only one thing which the Barrow people lack for meat and that is land game. Because they have settled down here in concentrated numbers for a very long time, they have killed off the land game and fished the inland lakes dry of fish throughout a large area. To particularize on why our Beechey Point people felt no desire to live amid the city attractions of Barrow, it was not only meat which they felt they would lack there, but their beloved caribou meat. Giving up the caribou meat would be, they felt, too great a hardship. It is a rare caribou which can be found anywhere near Point Barrow.

The long miles of naval stores passed by and scattered habitations of human beings appeared in front of our bow through the dismal skies and softly falling snow that are typical weather for Point Barrow the year through. Dora said to Connie in soft, sibilant Eskimo tones, as we all stood on the moving bow: "There is Barrow Village."

Beechey Point

Lieutenant Henry Ray of the International Polar Expedition to Point Barrow, 1881 to 1884, is seldom recalled today as the young explorer who set up the first observation station here. Since his time, Barrow has served as a base for many a forgotten expedition for something or other, and many are the diverse characters who have stood on its barren site.

Charlie Brower's trading post came into sight first. Charlie had been entertained once with some of his part Eskimo children in the White House in Washington as guest of Theodore Roosevelt; the old man died the year before our visit. Although Charlie is gone fourteen grown children survive, several of them now rearing families of their own in the

U. S. One is a brigadier general. Dave Brower and Tom Brower, sons, still manage the trading post of their father. The lagoon came, and then the new government hospital for the Eskimos, rebuilt since a fire had demolished it in 1937. The old government schoolhouse followed closely the largest outpost school for natives which we had seen in Alaska-but with outmoded, ramshackle, drafty quarters for the resident teachers. Then the residences of the natives scattered along. There were frame houses, tents, and shacks. Some of these Eskimo shacks contained radios blaring out the latest news commentaries from around the world. The United States "Weather Bureau houses in dark green added a clannish air as they nestled with their connecting boardwalks in a group apart. Each unit is said to have cost $20,000 to build in order to have small, modem, habitable living quarters for personnel.

The Presbyterian Church raised its steeple bravely into the sky, and rang a fine bell for it was Sunday morning. Church steeples always look friendly, somehow, no matter how gloomy the sky or how desolate the spot on earth where they rise, for they give at least the promise of permanence and stability so wanting in the very outline of all these other structures of a hurried, disorganized, and growing community.

Our boats passed all these things and grounded to a stop at the beach below the Native Store. We and all our Eskimos piled out. Behind us, a few hundred yards, lay the polar ice pack. It is always within plain sight right off Barrow, and sometimes it even comes close in with such ponderous force and towering pinnacles and ridges of ice formed by pressure in a wind that it may actually threaten to slice across the land and obliterate the little human settlement from the earth. Yet it has never quite done so; the ice has always managed to ground itself in time. We stepped ashore dizzily and realized that although Point Barrow was actually little farther north in latitude than our own Beechey Point, its climate was much more hostile, in conjunction with the fact that vegetation is almost entirely absent here and snow may fall through out any month of the year.

Every outsider who arrives at Barrow must come in either by the single yearly supply ship, which was now fighting its way through ice two hundred miles to the south past the Sea Horse Islands, or, as is more common today, on Sig Wein's Airlines. Therefore, each white visitor to the community is known before his arrival or within an hour after it, certainly. We were probably the first white people in a long time to arrive via the Arctic Ocean with a group of traveling Eskimos from the one unexpected direction the eastward. At first, not knowing just what we should do with ourselves, now that we were here, we dumbly followed our Eskimo companions to see where they went in the town. We didn't know a soul at the strange farthest north outpost. The Eskimos had left a tent behind at Beechey Point and we saw now that another tent was their destination at the end of their long trip. It must have been the sight of another tent which brought us to our senses, just as we started to crawl into it on hands and knees with the others.

We didn't belong with the Eskimos here, to drink from infected coffee cups the brew which had almost killed us, what with no water to drink for five days. We clung together dizzily and demurred. Then we politely excused ourselves from our good friends, probably to their own relief, and sought our own kind. A vacation was in order. We were going to call on white people!

7

Point BARROW is memorized by our school children as being the farthest north point of land on the North American continent, and it is for this of course that it has become famous. As with many famous bits of knowledge, however, we find that this belief is not altogether correct. It seems that over Canada way there is a place called Boothia Felix which for a long time was believed to be an island, but which some people now regard as a peninsula, and as a part of the mainland of the continent Boothia Felix stretches farther north than Point Barrow. Few people have been there. Boothia is the location of the Magnetic North Pole on our earth, but the Pole moves about, often as much as two hundred miles within a short time, so that it is difficult to put our finger on it. You could probably float a canoe or a small sailing boat over the Magnetic North Pole right across the neck of the Boothia peninsula when the water is high to make the "islands" at certain times if you wanted to!

The school principal at Barrow Village, Mr. Leon Vincent, who possesses an incurable sense of adventure about these things, told us that he and his wife had considered it when they were younger. They had originally come to Alaska bringing their first small child along with them, in their own sailing boat, several years ago. The Leon Vincents were the most outstanding people we visited at that time at Barrow; they would certainly be outstanding anywhere. We all had the same kind of hobbies, you might say.

Both the missionary and the physician of the community were absent when we arrived there. The missionary and his wife had just gone to Iran.

We stayed part of the time with some of the young couples who were in the cute little Weather Bureau houses, and they were very wonderful to us.

The weather at Point Barrow changes hourly. You can report clear, sleet, fog, rain, snow, and hail all in an hour. It's no joke, either, but an irritating reality to the people who try to check and report meteorological conditions. The United States Weather Bureau at Point Barrow is doing a work of importance because it is located in the far north west, and weather for our whole continent comes from the north and west. Point Barrow is farther west than the Hawaiian Islands; it is almost to Asia. The weather which Point Barrow has today is, in a measure, what the more southerly parts of our world may expect tomorrow or next week. This is weather taken at high altitudes, not on the ground. At the time we visited here the reports from Point Barrow were relayed to determine the military campaigns in the South Pacific.

It was at Point Barrow that Connie and I learned, first from the traveling Eskimos, and later from white people and their confirming radios and publications, of the two little bombs which were dropped upon Japan. The world had entered the Atomic Age!

Early in the season three big Liberty ships had made their way into Barrow from the North Pacific via the Bering Sea and Bering Strait and had unloaded the Navy's winter supplies. The Liberty ships had trouble with the ice, to be sure, but here one of the new improvements of arctic navigation among floating ice cakes was demonstrated. The ships had used Sig Wein in his airplane to spot the channels ahead through the ice, and the information about ice conditions was radioed to them. Thus. they were able to travel whenever an open lead allowed. In this way the Liberty ships had been able to come in to Point Barrow and unload and leave at an early date in August. Yet the old North Star, which had formerly been to the South Pole with Byrd and upon which the civilians in this part of the world now depended, was still held up some two hundred miles to the south by the heavy ice, and the month was September with freeze-up time imminent for the Arctic Ocean again.

We had been waiting at Barrow restlessly for several days when on September 11, just as we had heard that she never could make it this year, the good old North Star rounded the corner and hove into sight among the ice. For two days previous the ice had been nearly out of sight upon the horizon. Sig finally plotted a course for the North Star to follow through the ice. The pack had moved out before the village, leaving a ridge of grounded ice which could not get off. Between this ridge of ice and the shore lay some six hundred yards of open water. The North Star had to travel perhaps ten miles on past the town proper and up the point to get around the grounded ice and then work its way back between it and the shore.

The water was not very deep where the ice had grounded. The North Star made her way up this channel until within perhaps five miles of Barrow proper. Here she went aground, and the unloading began. The Native Store and the Navy furnished launches to tow the small clumsy barges from ship to town to unload. Everybody was grinning from ear to ear. The kids and the old people worked alike. Labor paid from fifty cents an hour for the very young on up to a dollar an hour for men. The men who operated the boats got more. As a barge came to shore everyone pitched in to unload it. The goods were piled hastily on the beach. The Native Store had an RD-6 Caterpillar and a drag sled to haul its supplies from the sandy beach to the storehouse.

Little Eskimo kids waded into the ice water dressed in all manner of shoes and skin water boots. They climbed upon small cakes of ice and pushed each other into the deeper water. They were sopping wet most of the time, while the temperature hung at freezing or just below. I greeted Mr. Vincent one morning: "Getting colder every day."

"Yes, it took two boys to break the ice in a puddle, so they could all get their feet wet this morning," he replied.

The stores at Barrow for the natives stock the essentials and I mean essentials nothing more. There wasn't a single item of canned fruits or vegetables to be had from the North Star for the Native Store only flour, sugar, canned milk, coffee, tea, shells, gasoline, kerosene, cartridges, and a very little cloth for snow shirts and dresses. There were also some things for the coal mine that the Eskimos were trying to operate with some success about seventy miles from Barrow. To call the selection scanty is putting it mildly. Yet the people were overjoyed. They had been out of everything for a long time. As Connie put it, "When you've got tea in this country, you're well off, but when you've got sugar to put in it-boy, you're rich!" Here in a nutshell lies the whole essence of the extent of civilized food in this part of the world.

Connie and I had long since found that there was no way we could buy food at Barrow other than from the Native Store, and there seemed to be a technical difficulty to overcome there, inasmuch as we were not Eskimos and the Native Store was for Eskimos only. Yet we could not obtain food from any of the white people, aside from what we ate as their temporary house guests, as they all got their own food from their own commissary and had none left over to spare. Of course, they were not allowed to sell their own commissary food anyway. There were no other stores and no hotel, although stores and hotels were expected to attract a postwar tourist trade at Barrow, what with the private airlines now running to bring tourists in. As a matter of fact, we did see one tourist while we were there-a traveling schoolteacher, and she took Abraham's picture as well as pictures of those same Point Barrow Eskimos all the visiting press reporters always get. Those same Eskimos have been photographed many times. Meantime, Connie and I wrangled with the busy and excited Native Store manager to find out if we could or could not obtain any food for the winter. It was not hard to guess that Beechey Point was on rations and that whatever we ate from Beechey Point supplies would mean so much less for Abraham to dole out to the others.

Here were other white people about us, living in houses, arriving by airplanes, regularly serviced with fresh foods by airplane at 62 cents for the pound. The village at Point Barrow lies 520 air miles from Fairbanks. The only fresh plums Connie and I actually got hold of in five years' residence in Alaska came from a Point Barrow resident's household refrigerator!

Now, were we not a little queer to see only the "wild" side of Alaska of which most of these newcomers see little? Will our tales not give the wrong impression of it? What accounted for these people living in a civilized way at remote Point Barrow, for instance, and for our having no home but the tents of the Eskimos?

We can only explain it by saying that the side of Alaska which you will hear described by people who work for government bureaus is the side which is probably most practical and most applicable for you. The point is that all these people are able to come here only by importing their own environment with them in prefabricated lots wherever they

Beechey Point

go. It costs some governmental or private agency thousands of dollars to maintain just one man and his family in the arctic in the degree of comfort and luxury which modern people demand, and without which they would not consider going there. They have business there which confines them to the spot. They are taken in and brought out again at the end of their term by air, and they know little of the rest of the country as the result of their stay. Despite the fact that any one who has lived at all in Alaska invariably considers himself the last word and expert in the subject of "Alaska," often a person does not know the conditions of his natural environment even at his very doorstep. Connie and I lived and traveled as we did in order to get really to know the country and its natives as a person living secluded in one house or village can rarely know them.

By September 23 Connie and I had long since been ready to leave for Beechey Point. Civilians and navy personnel alike had shown us a fine time, but extended hospitality in view of the uncertainties of freeze-up facing you can be a strain on hosts and obligatory guests alike. When would our Eskimos ever decide they had had enough of city life and get out of here while the getting was good? If a contract crew from the United States had done the unloading and sorting of the cargo of the North Star at Barrow, we could have been moving in five days at the most. But the Eskimos are a happy go-lucky lot. The ice was freezing every day, yet Sunday was a day of rest. Missionaries had taught the Eskimos the observance of the Sabbath. It has been observed by writers before we came along that at Barrow during the brief whaling season the Eskimos would often let a whale go by unmolested if it were a Sunday and would thus jeopardize their food supply for the entire ensuing winter-so seriously do they take Sunday in these parts!

The powerful crane that swung the gas drums from the beach, the weasels that shot past while almost hourly a PBY glided toward the big runways, contrasted strangely with a scrawly team of dogs driven by a poor Eskimo in a costume of mixed G.I. castoffs and a group of urchins who picked up things from the garbage dump. An amphibious tank was silhouetted against the incoming ice pack as the North Star sneaked out a few hours after she was unloaded.

The day came when our fleet of four cargo boats, towing the whaleboat, put out for the eastern ocean. Connie and I hadn't been able to get a radio for our house at Beechey Point, but we had got a portable phonograph and some records. I reflected on the condition of our fleet as I tried to hold a steady course. Behind came two boats tied together. One had already developed engine trouble. I throttled down while the third boat tied alongside its stricken companion. Blue smoke filled the air behind the limping team.

The hulls of the old boats were of soft wood, chafed and worn. The engines of the cargo boats had been run by first one man and then another who knew nothing about them. They smoked and limped along. There wasn't a single light on any of the craft except the gasoline lantern. the nights were black as all get-out now. Why weren't these boats equipped with searchlights? Why didn't we have tin or hard wood on the hulls to plow the young ice we knew we would meet? All these questions tumbled through my mind as we headed for Cape Halkett.

At Cape Simpson there is what the Eskimos call "pitch."

It is really an oil seep. Here they sometimes dig this pitch on the Naval Petroleum Reserve and sack it up. It makes a fine hot fire like burning oil, but as Abraham put it, you have to use a lot of wood along with it too, because "it is fierce on stoves." The high temperature it generates when burned in a sheet-iron stove eats the stove up.

We turned in to Cape Simpson to pick up a few sacks of pitch that had been dug many years ago. The sun as low in the northwest, turning the ocean rose and blue as we passed a single pinnacled floating ice cake, arch-shaped from the hole melted through the middle of it. Suddenly, an actual wild polar bear was discovered; he was swimming, and our boat fleet had overtaken him. It was rather unusual to find a polar bear swimming so far from his home on the main ice pack near land in the summer. He might have been just a piece of moving ice himself, when of the Eskimos on one of the other boats discovered him.

Of course, the swimming polar bear didn't have a chance. Rifles cracked, and bullets splashed about him, for all the boats rushed to the center of the excitement, and everyone had his rifle. Mine lay in its case in the bow and I left it there, for the Eskimos of the other boat had shot the bear almost more quickly than it takes to tell. At fifty yards the bear was killed by a shot which hit it in the brain, after an expenditure of some forty or fifty excited shots. The Eskimos were flush now.

The dead bear floated like a white cake of ice. The other boat put a rope around its neck and towed it up to the beach at Cape Simpson

Here a half dozen men lifted the bear up on deck. While some loaded the ten sacks of pitch for which we had stopped, the rest cut up the bear with their little pocketknives. Each boat got a piece. The hide would not be salable on the market since the bear was secured during the wrong season. In half an hour we were underway again. Polar bear ribs boiled over the primus stove and the sun rolled below the horizon.

We ate polar bear meat and drank tea in the glow of a swinging gasoline lantern as the boat churned on its way. From across the water came the flicker of other lanterns as we started across Smith Bay.

The darkness thickened; I could no longer read the compass card on the boat I was steering. From time to time a large cake of ice would gleam for a moment directly ahead. By putting the wheel hard over we would shave by with a few feet to spare. A sharp breeze sprang up and snow flurries began to blow. The breeze was a good thing because a still night would mean a freeze. Abraham came above and relieved me at the wheel.

I stood for a few moments thinking. Small ice cakes the size of a streetcar would leap from the darkness and fade just as quickly behind. The small lights of their boats strung out behind us. It was sixty miles to shore and there was floating ice everywhere. Not heavy ice, but ice scattered as miniature icebergs. If we hit one of those things traveling at full speed, we would burst open like an egg. Abraham grumbled about someone always giving orders to keep traveling. I knew what he felt. I felt the same way too, but the fellow from the Barrow Store in command had to return to Barrow, so I could see his side, too.

The crowd was all asleep when I went below. I made a bunk of a grizzly bear skin and stretched out. Thump! Scrape! Crunch! We struck a small cake of ice probably as big as a bushel basket, and my stomach turned over. It had gone back and struck the propeller. Apparently, no damage had been done, for the engine kept on with its steady rhythm. So, the miles of treacherous darkness slid beneath our bow–Smith Bay, Harrison Bay, moments counting against the freeze-up. Would we be stuck in the ice? On the far side of Harrison Bay, a family came out to meet us in their whaleboat, to trade. We tied up to a cake of ice there where everyone leisurely talked and stretched and used the arctic toilet.

On September 23 we anchored off Oliktok. Night fell, and a storm seemed imminent. A party was in order. All throughout the night the coffeepot boiled, and the biscuits flowed freely. The moon rose tulip red out of the naked arctic land. In the early morning we found ourselves aground. Of course, the Eskimos had not worried about the obvious fact that with an offshore wind the tide would drop and leave us dry with our heavy load. For hours we all pushed and pulled with long poles. Then, after waiting a day more, the tide swelled full again, and we floated off. Four hours later we were at Beechey Point. There was a shelf of ice extending out from shore some fifty yards, but we were able to batter our way through it slowly until the bow of the leading boat grounded on bottom; then we jumped off the bow onto the shelf ice and were able to walk ashore.

Home for the winter! The grass was brown and the prairie stretching inland from the old trading post was devoid of flowers, while the fresh-water lakes were already frozen into iron to walk upon. There were only a few human beings to welcome us on the beach. That was funny only George and Nanny and their family and Ada and her girls were left. Where were the others?

A party was held in the big house next door to us the night of our return. The visitors from Barrow were treated to the best, and we expect that a good time was had by all. They had the only lamp, so we went to bed.

When we awoke the next morning, the sky was gray and fine snowflakes were blowing diagonally past the window panes. I remember the queer feeling which gripped us for a moment when Connie ran out of the door and back in again breathlessly, to exclaim, "They're gone!"

The rolling Arctic Ocean out beyond the shelf ice which extended before Beechey Point was empty. The Barrow Eskimos had taken the cargo boats and left in the night. Like the birds, they had got away at precisely the last moment before the ocean closed.

Well, it was only for a year! We couldn't know the wonderful and unusual adventures that were ahead. We were getting what we had asked for. We were left on the arctic coast of Alaska with the Eskimos for the winter.

PART FOUR

The Coming of Winter

After freeze up, families depart for winter camps

We carry water to Beechey Point as winter descend

1

We had come to live at Beechey Point under the impression that we were taking up residence in a settled community. We had come to live with the Eskimos. Yet when we returned to Beechey Point from Point Barrow there were scarcely any people left about. Nobody had told us that most of the people, having got a few supplies from the first boats, would have already left for parts unknown. Most of these people here even now would be scattered to the winds before the week.

So, this was why the Eskimos put in no winter's fuel! They would gather only enough sticks to burn day by day, and when that was gone in one locality they would merely pack up and move to another place where wood was!

Somehow the summer had gone, we had gathered no fuel for winter with which to heat our house, and the fact was presently made clear that no caribou skins had been secured for us as promised by George Woods's family, while the hair of existent living animals now was too long for properly fitting clothing. Richard's People had got a good many skins, but we found this out too late, and the skins were sold to Barrow for the higher prices.

How would we haul fuel? We needed a dog team. Abraham suggested that perhaps we could hire George to get his oldest son, Apiak, to keep us in wood for a while. The other family would be living nearby for a few weeks yet. I walked down the beach to their tent, listened to a long story, drank some tea. "The main thing is to get dog feed," said George. "I have no feed for my dogs." By dog feed George meant seals. But all seals should have been secured before the ocean started to freeze, and it was too late for sealing now. Like most of the other Eskimos, George subsequently fed his dogs almost altogether on caribou during the ensuing winter. Not a person in the village had gone seal hunting after we left for Barrow. Nobody had hunted all summer. The women played achichigok all through the long summer days instead of tanning the ugrug hides. The people sang hymns and entertained Andrew the minister from Barter Island. His stay of several weeks kept our seamstress Nanny so busy cooking for the hordes of visitors and presiding as a lady of fashion that she had taken no time to sew. Now she was behind on her winter sewing for her own family.

But George agreed to have Apiak bring a little wood soon for our immediate needs until I could think what to do further, as we had only two days' supply of wood to burn when we got home. The wood must be hauled a dozen miles, and this was why we could not get it ourselves. The ensuing months told us that all of the Eskimos we dealt with are meticulously honest and that they have the best intentions in the world, yet if you wait for them to bring you your wood you will count every stick that you put in the stove; it is the frustrating conditions of Eskimo environment which have in all likelihood trained them in the course of time not to worry much about anything. You have to thoroughly understand the conditions of this environment and live in it yourself if you are ever going to understand the Eskimo personality.

When the Woods family all came down with colds which were contracted from the visitors from Point Barrow, Connie said to me: "I think it's all your fault. When you were out hunting ugrugs all during those summer days, why weren't you getting wood? You're no example to the Eskimos. You should have hired them to lay in our wood as any white person in his right mind would have done."

I tried to explain to Connie that it had seemed best to get ugrugs for boot soles first and that every day we had all been waiting for the return of the cargo boat from Barrow, since without this boat and gasoline in the village there was no economical way to haul wood during the summer at all. You just burned it faster than you could accumulate it. Connie was afraid that we wouldn't be able to find wood after the snows came, but I wasn't worried about that just annoyed.

I had learned enough about the arctic beaches already to know that wood can be kicked out of the snow easily enough at any season along the edge of the ocean. The snowfall in the arctic is not heavy, and usually wood is exposed by the winds. Our first snow had not yet fallen, and the month of September had passed.

Could we hire Abraham to help us out with his own dog team in hauling wood? No, he believed his dog team could not do more than supply his own house this winter, he said. Could we buy a dog team and sled of our own, then?' We had already thought of this expedient and earnestly desired to have a dog team. But it did not seem likely. By fall the Eskimos had none to spare; I could make a sled, but dogs were not obtainable.

"Why don't you give Abraham a good talking to?" Connie cried. "Why, if it weren't for our motor and gasoline, he and Dora wouldn't even have got to Barrow to get married! Think of all our grub they ate up!"

I did talk to him. It only made him nervous and he smoked cigarettes faster than ever. He was a good guy at heart. It was merely that the women of his household nagged him at times, and, being a newly married man, he was somewhat preoccupied so that he hated to think about practical matters. In fact, one of the absent-minded things he did was to leave our little sheet-iron stove at Barrow by accident; we never saw it again. Presently I made another one similar to it at Beechey Point out of a 55-gallon oil drum. It had a little oven for baking and burned sticks about sixteen inches long in the firebox.

"We must learn to get along with the Eskimos, or else we are a failure on this coast and our whole experiment of trying to learn about Eskimos will be a total loss," we told ourselves in our moments of discouragement. Like a maiden whose suitor has dropped her hand all too eagerly when some obstacle looms, I knew that I had better offer encouragement and try to arouse the other's confidence in himself or I would lose him altogether. Abraham looked foolish and sneaking whenever I saw him. He had kept all the "pitch" from Cape Simpson, saying that its use was supposed to be to heat the "store." Connie and I resurrected the old ice cream freezer found on the floor of the dog shed and we turned it and made ice cream from precious ice cream powder we had secured through friends at Point Barrow. Abraham and Dora, looking timid and uneasy, turned up at our unheated house, induced by the promise of ice cream and cigars. The box of cigars had been presented us in all kindness by the people at Barrow. Some of the tension was relieved by our ridiculous ice cream and cigar party, and Abraham went home happier and we felt a little happier, too.

It was on the first day of November that Connie got her own parka made from the two young bull skins I had secured last summer, and presently we each had complete arctic outfits to the point where we could at least get by very nicely.

These things having materialized from Nanny's skillful hands, we found our fears about lack of fuel curiously diminished. With a warm parka on our backs we even began gradually to partake of some of the Eskimo's nonchalance about fuel-that most necessary of all substances of existence to the white man in arctic climes. If we couldn't heat our house altogether, what matter now? Even when George and Nanny and all of their family and the widow Ada and her girls left together, with three dog teams, traveling along the edge of the ocean towards fall "fish camp" at the mouth of the Colville River some thirty-five miles away, we could rejoice in their pleasure as we watched them go. The prairie by the side of the frozen ocean was brown and there was yet no snow. The dogs' feet, gripping the crystalline sea ice which shelved out from shore towards the gray waves, left bloody prints behind. The families of Eskimos, with little crippled Martha riding at the fore-Martha was very popular with all the teen-age girls—all piled on top of the sleds with shouts of joy over the first ride of the season. We stood in our parkas beside our house on that bleak sere shore feeling suddenly almost independent of Nanny, and watched her go.

Abraham, Dora, and Thelma continued to live next door for a time. They were the only family left. Two caribou wandered by the houses and Abraham shot them, using the new telescope on his rifle successfully. Dora brought one of the tongues over to Connie as a gift, along with a big dried apple pie. Dora and Thelma up on top of the trading post watched for ptarmigan and stalked the birds with a .22 rifle. The Eskimo girls were good hunters and would always sit down to shoot in order to take a steady rest over their knees for hitting the mark. I have seldom seen an Eskimo shoot offhand standing up.

We held a washday for the present and amused ourselves similarly. I packed thirty gallons of water from the inland lake a quarter of a mile away, we borrowed washtubs and washboard from Dora; Connie rubbed on our old pants and shirts and underwear until her hands got sore and then I took a try at it. On the second day we finished our washing. The steam from the drying wash inside the house clung to the walls in drops of water, condensing on these cold surfaces. The water ran down the walls in rivers and streams, while even our bedding became soaked with clammy sweat. The wash took five days to dry and we realized from the one experiment that we would not really wash a number of clothes again for the rest of this year that is, if we meant to preserve our lives and health.

When Abraham's family left for fish camp later, we happened to see their preparations from the window, so we went outside and waved them off. Dogs howled and danced in approval, plumed tails waving. Abraham's dogs were in wonderful condition; he possesses an admirable team, the largest, the strongest, and the speediest dogs on all this coast-or so we had heard before now from George. The last we saw of the family was where their sled vanished with a thump over the bank and down onto the sea ice. And we had never ridden with a dog team yet!

Thus, we found ourselves the sole inhabitants of Beechey Point when we had come here on purpose to live with the Eskimos! At this season every Eskimo east of Point Barrow goes to the Colville River delta to fish with nets underneath the ice. The wind blew ceaselessly, banging the clapboards on the sides of the house, while the primus stove we had been able to borrow from Abraham was enabled, by burning a quart of gasoline in eight hours, to keep out the worst of the chill. Sometimes we danced to the portable phonograph, but it would freeze solid at the temperatures we soon came to take for granted inside the house. About once in every five days Connie and I would push an empty sled out across the sea ice to the near-by shore some four miles away and spend the day getting wood. The outdoor exercise didn't do us any harm, as a matter of fact. We continued to be in splendid health. What's more, I was beginning to have an idea that we wouldn't be just sitting here in this house all winter. It was not what we came for.

It was not long thereafter that in the thick-flying snow near dark of eve one day Abraham came visiting from thirtyfive miles. He was supposed to service himself as well as other people who wanted supplies from the warehouse, but he forgot his keys so had to chop the lock off the trading post with an ax. He was just having supper with us when

Apiak, with Pete, Ada's oldest boy, blew in. We all had a jolly meal of boiled ptarmigan followed by smokes for them and the Victrola. The house was warm because they brought the wood. They got five dollars the dog-sled load for it. Outside our lighted window-lighted by the kerosene lantern we had managed to get hold of sleds were parked upside down and three dog teams slept in the snow. Inside there were music and Eskimo laughter. The Eskimos were getting used to us in time. It is curious that none ever abused our hospitality. They would remain perhaps one hour after supper, never more. Suddenly, when they felt the time had come to go, they merely got up and went out. We usually had to close the door behind them as they never seemed conscious of the fact that we might want to keep the house warm. Darkskinned men of the open, tanned from the drifting snow, their step-in deerskin boots was light and graceful, but they were uneasy about walking in and out of houses, and didn't know what to do.

One of the things Connie had a theory about was the taste of primitive people in music. What kind of musical instruments will a human being prefer if he has never heard any music before? Will he like his music sweet or will he like it, as we say, hot? Will he like the so-called classical music and appreciate, if he has not been corrupted, the symphonies of the great masters? Here one might make a deduction as to how well "instinct" is a factor in guiding our musical choice, if one could find out what kind of music the really primitive person likes, thought Connie. She held onto a hope that the Eskimos would naturally take to the "finer things" as heard on our Victrola.

We had Count Basie's boogie-woogie and the "Grand Canyon Suite." There was a whole book of Strauss waltzes, and Lily Pons operated on the high C frequency on some of our records while Ginny Simms got tropical with the more Latin tunes. Tommy Dorsey's orchestra placed emphasis on the brass while the Three Suns were tuneful enough with the electric organ. We had a little of everything in our musical repertoire.

The Eskimos soon learned to operate the phonograph and were, of course, welcome to do so. They were very careful not to wind it too tight, and often it would run down in the middle of a piece with awful results, but you might say these were merely their mechanical difficulties with it; we managed to keep our hands off it most of the time.

In visiting our house, the people chose their own records to play, and of course picked them at first at random. They could not read the titles, but by chance they would hit upon some kind of music which pleased them, and this record was at once identified by some sign known only to the Eskimo himself. Eskimos are an extremely observant people when it comes to small details in the structure of anything, so that by a second visit each person knew the records with which he had experimented almost as well as we knew them by reading their titles. Unerringly the visitor would dive to the bottom of the pile, if need be, and would come up with one record first and last. It did not take the whole north coast of Alaska very long to find it-the slowest, most monotonous and mournful of cowboy ballads describing a lost love which I ever hope to hear again in my life. The Eskimos could not understand the words; not even Abraham got them until we explained. Yet this music had some message for these people. For some reason unknown to me it was the kind of music they understood, and the only kind folk music arising from the early pioneer spirit of our old South or, west. It is repetitious, has a very, very simple, sad, and yet harmonious refrain, perhaps because it has originated from just plain people rather than from some sophisticated composer. We found the Eskimos do not rise to even simple modern jazz, let alone boogie-woogie, for boogie-woogie is really very sophisticated compared to folk music! As for symphonies, they are completely beyond the Eskimos, as they are beyond most of us. But just how the Eskimos palpitated for that sad cowboy alone with his horse on a prairie we learned during a year of hearing that single favorite record.

Not until the last week in October did we get a single below-zero temperature; now the beautiful pinks and blues which are so characteristic of the long arctic winter began to be here with us. Ptarmigan walking the flawless drifts beside the trading post cackled like chickens. Ptarmigan seen thus look almost pale pink, when you stare hard through slitted lids against the glare of an all-white world. The white grouse pop out of the landscape about you and have that delicate pink glow of a pearl that is held up to the light. I went into the house and got the shotgun and my parka in one grab. thought a few extra birds in the larder wouldn't do any harm, for a few weeks from now would find them all migrated some miles inland from the coast to where the taller willows grow, so I had learned.

So, I went after the covey which surrounded the buildings, not for the first or the last time. As the first cackling white bird flashed past me in the air, I got him with one shot, but it took three salutes to get the second as it sailed far out. Only two birds actually out of that flock—and then the three hundred or so which had come into our front yard and which I hadn't seen against the snow had whirred away and gone! We spent the day picking birds and developing some pictures. I made Connie two new baking pans and she was as happy over them as a kid with a new toy. Of such simple things as these is day-by-day life composed in arctic regions.

By November and December, the air was full of flying snow, but it was only fine powder picked up from the prairie and carried a hundred miles before each grain would find its resting place. The flying snow stings your eyes and freezes on your cheeks, imposing special difficulties in travel. We learned to travel always with a tail wind. The Eskimos actually call a blizzard their best traveling day, and no blizzard, if it happens to be going their way, is too fierce to keep them at home. Mistaken naturalists have sometimes tried to describe these blizzards in books by stating that in the arctic no living thing can remain out in them and stay alive. But we know that the adapted animal of the arctic weathers many such a gale during a single season, and as for the Eskimos, never having possessed a weather thermometer, they have no scale of measurement for how cold it is, while they in fact like a high wind, since they will merely put a big sail on their sled, smile their broadest smile, jump on, and hold tight. Yes, Eskimos sometimes have frozen to death through some accident or other, but this is not often; even frostbite as we know it in other climates is completely unfamiliar.

One of the interesting features about our home beside the Arctic Ocean was that we could always look out our window any time of day and see game unexpectedly. Near evening when we had been reading all day a female Pacific eider duck came flopping along our way, and I noticed from the window where I sat that one of those big lazy snowy owls was following it. The two came to a landing on the prairie a quarter of a mile away. The owl, I noticed, sat a little apart from the duck. One of nature's quaint friendships of the kind we hear in children's stories? No, I wish that it were. When I went over, the owl flew away, but the duck sat still. "It's sick. I knew it." Just as I reached down to pick the duck up, it flopped off out of my reach and began to fly. At this point I shot it because I knew I would never otherwise catch it, and the merciful thing should be done. While I had never been around eiders or lived on the arctic prairie before, any farm boy would know that this solitary duck left alone in a frozen world spelled only one answer: disaster for the duck. When I retrieved the pitiful creature, I found that its feet and bill were frozen solid. The emaciated body beneath the feathers instantly told me of starvation. There was nothing left here now for a water-feeding duck to eat.

Why had it stayed behind? Why had it not migrated? Perhaps it had been wounded early in the summer by shot from some Eskimo's shotgun around Beechey Point. Or perhaps it had matured late for it was a this year's bird-and had not known where to go. Whatever had caused it to linger, it had stayed around the entrance of some stream or river into the Arctic Ocean where the water kept open until the last. But daily its feeding pond grew smaller, and when its companions left, apparently it could not fly southward with them.

But it could fly now. From this and similar instances there seems some reason to believe, then, that birds may not all have the "instinct" to migrate south or do not know where to go unless the old birds are there to show them the way. If a duck born this summer is not with old birds or becomes separated from them, he does not seem to know what to do or where to go, but flies back and forth over the frozen arctic looking for the water which is nonexistent until the inevitable end overtakes him. It seems probable also that there are some weak birds which are not able to make the trip southward. I saw a flock of a dozen eiders as late as December. They flew along the frozen shore line following their ancient ancestral routes, looking, no doubt, for open water. One bird was lagging far behind; he couldn't keep up.

An Eskimo man came in one day from far up the Colville and Itkillik Rivers, from near Chandler Lake. The man brought skins to trade with Abraham. I hung around and watched the procedure. He had twenty dollars. With this he bought twenty-five pounds of flour, one carton of cigarettes, ten plugs of chewing tobacco, one carton of matches, one box of .30-30 shells, a new shirt, a pound of rope, a box of baking soda (he would make sourdough biscuits with the flour), and some oatmeal. He had also bought a pound of coffee, but he couldn't pay for it, so this had to be left behind. Abraham deals with no long-term credit; the terms are harsh, but one supposes unavoidably so in dealing with these people. Then back over the hundreds of miles with his purchases on his dog sled the Eskimo hunter started.

A man and a woman with a small child at breast came with their sled and five dogs from the eastward, and went on towards Barrow.

The sun now made but a small arc in the south, dropped, and the short day was over. There was good light from 8 A.M. to 5 P.M. because there was a long twilight while the sun rolled along just below the rim of the world. Mirages circled the horizon of the frozen ocean while little puffs of vaporous clouds filled the skies on a clear day like antiaircraft bursts. After the ocean froze the steel-cold sky remained perfectly clear as a rule except for a fog bank which might hang low in the distance over the frozen sea. Fogs by winter are said to be seen only along the margin of the continent. They usually do not occur either inland on the prairies or outward at sea. Polar aviation is best by winter because the visibility is best then.

By November 16 we had three hours of sunlight daily. The presence of a slight haze or the mirage effects of cold clear weather we found can vastly influence the length of time the sun is visible at this season. Now the sun would but barely peep up in the south, would make a short roll along the white prairie, and then would drop again.

It took only a couple of days after that for the sun to disappear altogether for his midwinter sleep. The much dreaded "arctic night" of the white man had come. This period would last a little over two months in these latitudes and the main thing about it to us was that we would not be able to take colored pictures for a while. The time goes fast if one has some trips to take and sights to see.

For I had gathered from my occasional talks with Abraham that trips can be and are continually being taken during the arctic night by the light of the stars and the moon and the Northern Lights. And I had learned that despite all of the false rumors southerly people hear on this subject, there is not a time during the arctic night when there aren't four or five hours of twilight for traveling time each day!

We were going to have a dog team and sled of our own to go places with! I had never given up on that, for Connie and I had never been the kind just to sit in our house and not see anything of our environment. I had begun to realize, moreover, that we had little choice about it. We were going to have to leave our house. As the days grew colder and winter came on, we would have to give up our house at Beechey Point because we simply did not have the fuel to heat it. This worried me, but I tried to sound optimistic about it as I told Connie that we might go out with a hired hunter and dog team and camp out this winter in our tent.

"Our summer tent? Just our ordinary tent?" Connie gasped. "How can we live in a tent in the arctic in the winter time?"

"How do you suppose all of these Eskimos are living in one?" I countered. "I am beginning to get wise to them. They live in a tent—why of course!—because they have found that it is the most comfortable way in which to live in this country! It stands to reason that they can't have permanent residences because they would soon burn up all the fuel around any permanent residence. It's easier to move your house in this country to where the fuel is than to try to move the fuel to the house. For everything we have seen the Eskimos do thus far we have found that there is a reason behind it! Have you imagined that those Eskimos are cold and shivering out in their tents all this time? I'll tell you something—I'll bet you anything you want to bet that they are a whole lot more comfortable than we are right here in this house!"

Why, when we stopped to think about it, we even had a better tent than most of the Eskimos had. At least it didn't have holes in it. Our fur clothing was better and more complete than some of theirs. What were we crying about?

Abraham told me he thought we could hire a good boy with his dog team to live in our family and be our hunter and helper by paying him a monthly wage. Such a boy would convey us around with the sled and no more would we be helpless and tied to one spot! Like the Eskimos, we too could be mobile with our own household!

From such an Eskimo, I would learn myself how to make a warm camp in the snow. As a matter of fact, it was a fortunate thing that circumstances forced us to come to this to survive, or we would have missed an experience. Connie would come along too-there was no place else for her to stay. And I suppose if this had not been so, as a white man I would never have thought it possible to take my wife to live in a snow house. Hope dawned brightly for us as the sun sank.

Soon the moon made its red circle around the sky while the old trading post stood alone and desolate. The Eskimos and even we were gone. Gone where in the arctic? I recall that the last tip of the sun we saw during the old year was one elongated prong stuck above the snow so dimmed by mists that the sun looked for all the world just like a moon.

Connie Helmericks with daughter Jeanie, April 1952

About the Author

In 1942, at the age of twenty-four, Constance Helmericks and her husband, Bud Helmericks, paddled into the Alaskan wilds to live off the land. Over the next decade, Connie wrote five bestselling books on their adventures, and co-filmed and produced three documentaries with Bud. Their work was shown on national lecture tours, and was twice featured in LIFE magazine, including the cover. In her later books, Connie wrote of her wilderness journeys across Canada and around Australia with her young daughters, Jean and Ann Helmericks. She became an early environmental activist, walking much of the Pacific Crest trail alone while in her sixties. Connie was writing her ninth book about paddling Central American rivers when she died on Earth Day in 1987.

www.ingramcontent.com/pod-product-compliance
Lightning Source LLC
Chambersburg PA
CBHW050316120526
44592CB00014B/1930